Crosswalk Coach for the Common Core State Standards, English Language Arts, Grade 6

Triumph Learning®

Crosswalk Coach for the Common Core State Standards, English Language Arts, Grade 6
313NA
ISBN-13: 978-0-7836-7880-1

Contributing Writer: Kathy Furgang
Cover Image: © Veer/Image Source Photography

Triumph Learning® 136 Madison Avenue, 7th Floor, New York, NY 10016

Frequently Asked Questions about the Common Core State Standards

What are the Common Core State Standards?

The Common Core State Standards for mathematics and English language arts, grades K–12, are a set of shared goals and expectations for the knowledge and skills that will help students succeed. They allow students to understand what is expected of them and to become progressively more proficient in understanding and using mathematics and English language arts. Teachers will be better equipped to know exactly what they must do to help students learn and to establish individualized benchmarks for them.

Will the Common Core State Standards tell teachers how and what to teach?

No. Because the best understanding of what works in the classroom comes from teachers, these standards will establish *what* students need to learn, but they will not dictate *how* teachers should teach. Instead, schools and teachers will decide how best to help students reach the standards.

What will the Common Core State Standards mean for students?

The standards will provide a clear, consistent understanding of what is expected of student learning across the country. Common standards will not prevent different levels of achievement among students, but they will ensure more consistent exposure to materials and learning experiences through curriculum, instruction, teacher preparation, and other supports for student learning. These standards will help give students the knowledge and skills they need to succeed in college and careers.

Do the Common Core State Standards focus on skills and content knowledge?

Yes. The Common Core State Standards recognize that both content and skills are important. They require rigorous content and application of knowledge through higher-order thinking skills. The English language arts standards require certain critical content for all students, including classic myths and stories from around the world, America's founding documents, foundational American literature, and Shakespeare. The remaining crucial decisions about content are left to state and local determination. In addition to content coverage, the Common Core State Standards require that students systematically acquire knowledge of literature and other disciplines through reading, writing, speaking, and listening.

In mathematics, the Common Core State Standards lay a solid foundation in whole numbers, addition, subtraction, multiplication, division, fractions, and decimals. Together, these elements support a student's ability to learn and apply more demanding math concepts and procedures.

The Common Core State Standards require that students develop a depth of understanding and ability to apply English language arts and mathematics to novel situations, as college students and employees regularly do.

Will common assessments be developed?

It will be up to the states: some states plan to come together voluntarily to develop a common assessment system. A state-led consortium on assessment would be grounded in the following principles: allowing for comparison across students, schools, districts, states and nations; creating economies of scale; providing information and supporting more effective teaching and learning; and preparing students for college and careers.

Table of Contents

Common Core State Standards
W.6.1, W.6.10, WHST.6.1, WHST.6.10
W.6.2, W.6.10, WHST.6.2, WHST.6.10
W.6.3, W.6.10, WHST.6.10
W.6.4, W.6.5, W.6.6, WHST.6.4, WHST.6.5, WHST.6.6, L.6.3.a–b, L.6.6
W.6.7, W.6.8, WHST.6.7, WHST.6.8
L.6.1.a–d
L.6.2.a–b
L.6.4.a–b, L.6.5.b
L.6.4.c–d, L.6.5.c
L.6.1.e

Common Core State Standards Correlation Chart

Common Core State Standard	Grade 6	Crosswalk Coach Lesson(s)
Reading Standards for Literature		
Key Ideas and Details		
RL.6.1	Cite textual evidence to support analysis of what the text says explicitly as well as inferences drawn from the text.	7
RL.6.2	Determine a theme or central idea of a text and how it is conveyed through particular details; provide a summary of the text distinct from personal opinions or judgments.	3
RL.6.3	Describe how a particular story's or drama's plot unfolds in a series of episodes as well as how the characters respond or change as the plot moves toward a resolution.	1
Craft and Structure		
RL.6.4	Determine the meaning of words and phrases as they are used in a text, including figurative and connotative meanings; analyze the impact of a specific word choice on meaning and tone.	4
RL.6.5	Analyze how a particular sentence, chapter, scene, or stanza fits into the overall structure of a text and contributes to the development of the theme, setting, or plot.	5
RL.6.6	Explain how an author develops the point of view of the narrator or speaker in a text.	2
Integration of Knowledge and Ideas		
RL.6.7	Compare and contrast the experience of reading a story, drama, or poem to listening to or viewing an audio, video, or live version of the text, including contrasting what they "see" and "hear" when reading the text to what they perceive when they listen or watch.	N/A
RL.6.9	Compare and contrast texts in different forms or genres (e.g., stories and poems; historical novels and fantasy stories) in terms of their approaches to similar themes and topics.	6
Range of Reading and Level of Text Complexity		
RL.6.10	By the end of the year, read and comprehend literature, including stories, dramas, and poems, in the grades 6–8 text complexity band proficiently, with scaffolding as needed at the high end of the range.	1–7
Reading Standards for Informational Text		
Key Ideas and Details		
RI.6.1	Cite textual evidence to support analysis of what the text says explicitly as well as inferences drawn from the text.	7
RI.6.2	Determine a central idea of a text and how it is conveyed through particular details; provide a summary of the text distinct from personal opinions or judgments.	8
RI.6.3	Analyze in detail how a key individual, event, or idea is introduced, illustrated, and elaborated in a text (e.g., through examples or anecdotes).	9
Craft and Structure		
RI.6.4	Determine the meaning of words and phrases as they are used in a text, including figurative, connotative, and technical meanings.	11
RI.6.5	Analyze how a particular sentence, paragraph, chapter, or section fits into the overall structure of a text and contributes to the development of the ideas.	9
RI.6.6	Determine an author's point of view or purpose in a text and explain how it is conveyed in the text.	14

Common Core State Standard	Grade 6	Crosswalk Coach Lesson(s)
	**Reading Standards for Informational Text** *(continued)*	
	**Integration of Knowledge and Ideas**	
RI.6.7	Integrate information presented in different media or formats (e.g., visually, quantitatively) as well as in words to develop a coherent understanding of a topic or issue.	14
RI.6.8	Trace and evaluate the argument and specific claims in a text, distinguishing claims that are supported by reasons and evidence from claims that are not.	13
RI.6.9	Compare and contrast one author's presentation of events with that of another (e.g., a memoir written by and a biography on the same person).	14
	**Range of Reading and Level of Text Complexity**	
RI.6.10	By the end of the year, read and comprehend literary nonfiction in the grades 6–8 text complexity band proficiently, with scaffolding as needed at the high end of the range.	8–14
	**Writing Standards**	
	**Text Types and Purposes**	
W.6.1	Write arguments to support claims with clear reasons and relevant evidence. a. Introduce claim(s) and organize the reasons and evidence clearly. b. Support claim(s) with clear reasons and relevant evidence, using credible sources and demonstrating an understanding of the topic of the text. c. Use words, phrases, and clauses to clarify the relationships among claim(s) and reasons. d. Establish and maintain a formal style. e. Provide a concluding statement or section that follows from the argument presented.	15
W.6.2	Write informative/explanatory texts to examine a topic and convey ideas, concepts, and information through selection, organization, and analysis of relevant content. a. Introduce a topic; organize ideas, concepts, and information, using strategies such as definition, classification, comparison/contrast, and cause/effect; include formatting (e.g., headings), graphics (e.g., charts, tables), and multimedia when useful to aiding comprehension. b. Develop the topic with relevant facts, definitions, concrete details, quotations, or other information and examples. c. Use appropriate transitions to clarify the relationships among ideas and concepts. d. Use precise language and domain-specific vocabulary to inform about or explain the topic. e. Establish and maintain a formal style. f. Provide a concluding statement or section that follows from the information or explanation presented.	16
W.6.3	Write narratives to develop real or imagined experiences or events using effective technique, relevant descriptive details, and well-structured event sequences. a. Engage and orient the reader by establishing a context and introducing a narrator and/or characters; organize an event sequence that unfolds naturally and logically. b. Use narrative techniques, such as dialogue, pacing, and description, to develop experiences, events, and/or characters. c. Use a variety of transition words, phrases, and clauses to convey sequence and signal shifts from one time frame or setting to another. d. Use precise words and phrases, relevant descriptive details, and sensory language to convey experiences and events. e. Provide a conclusion that follows from the narrated experiences or events.	17

Common Core State Standard	Grade 6	Crosswalk Coach Lesson(s)
Writing Standards *(continued)*		
Production and Distribution of Writing		
W.6.4	Produce clear and coherent writing in which the development, organization, and style are appropriate to task, purpose, and audience. (Grade-specific expectations for writing types are defined in standards 1–3 above.)	18
W.6.5	With some guidance and support from peers and adults, develop and strengthen writing as needed by planning, revising, editing, rewriting, or trying a new approach. (Editing for conventions should demonstrate command of Language standards 1–3 up to and including grade 6.)	18
W.6.6	Use technology, including the Internet, to produce and publish writing as well as to interact and collaborate with others; demonstrate sufficient command of keyboarding skills to type a minimum of three pages in a single sitting.	18
Research to Build and Present Knowledge		
W.6.7	Conduct short research projects to answer a question, drawing on several sources and refocusing the inquiry when appropriate.	19
W.6.8	Gather relevant information from multiple print and digital sources; assess the credibility of each source; and quote or paraphrase the data and conclusions of others while avoiding plagiarism and providing basic bibliographic information for sources.	19
W.6.9	Draw evidence from literary and informational texts to support analysis, reflection, and research. a. Apply grade 6 Reading standards to literature (e.g., "Compare and contrast texts in different forms or genres [e.g., stories and poems; historical novels and fantasy stories] in terms of their approaches to similar themes and topics"). b. Apply grade 6 Reading standards to literary nonfiction (e.g., "Trace and evaluate the argument and specific claims in a text, distinguishing claims that are supported by reasons and evidence from claims that are not").	6, 14
Range of Writing		
W.6.10	Write routinely over extended time frames (time for research, reflection, and revision) and shorter time frames (a single sitting or a day or two) for a range of discipline-specific tasks, purposes, and audiences.	15–17
Language Standards		
Conventions of Standard English		
L.6.1	Demonstrate command of the conventions of standard English grammar and usage when writing or speaking. a. Ensure that pronouns are in the proper case (subjective, objective, possessive). b. Use intensive pronouns (e.g., *myself, ourselves*). c. Recognize and correct inappropriate shifts in pronoun number and person. d. Recognize and correct vague pronouns (i.e., ones with unclear or ambiguous antecedents). e. Recognize variations from standard English in their own and others' writing and speaking, and identify and use strategies to improve expression in conventional language.	20 20 20 20 24
L.6.2	Demonstrate command of the conventions of standard English capitalization, punctuation, and spelling when writing. a. Use punctuation (commas, parentheses, dashes) to set off nonrestrictive/parenthetical elements. b. Spell correctly.	21 21

Common Core State Standard	Grade 6	Crosswalk Coach Lesson(s)
	**Language Standards** *(continued)*	
	**Knowledge of Language**	
L.6.3	Use knowledge of language and its conventions when writing, speaking, reading, or listening. a. Vary sentence patterns for meaning, reader/listener interest, and style. b. Maintain consistency in style and tone.	 18 18
	**Vocabulary Acquisition and Use**	
L.6.4	Determine or clarify the meaning of unknown and multiple-meaning words and phrases based on *grade 6 reading and content*, choosing flexibly from a range of strategies. a. Use context (e.g., the overall meaning of a sentence or paragraph; a word's position or function in a sentence) as a clue to the meaning of a word or phrase. b. Use common, grade-appropriate Greek or Latin affixes and roots as clues to the meaning of a word (e.g., *audience, auditory, audible*). c. Consult reference materials (e.g., dictionaries, glossaries, thesauruses), both print and digital, to find the pronunciation of a word or determine or clarify its precise meaning or its part of speech. d. Verify the preliminary determination of the meaning of a word or phrase (e.g., by checking the inferred meaning in context or in a dictionary).	 22 22 23 23
L.6.5	Demonstrate understanding of figurative language, word relationships, and nuances in word meanings. a. Interpret figures of speech (e.g., personification) in context. b. Use the relationship between particular words (e.g., cause/effect, part/whole, item/category) to better understand each of the words. c. Distinguish among the connotations (associations) of words with similar denotations (definitions) (e.g., *stingy, scrimping, economical, unwasteful, thrifty*).	 4 22 23
L.6.6	Acquire and use accurately grade-appropriate general academic and domain-specific words and phrases; gather vocabulary knowledge when considering a word or phrase important to comprehension or expression.	18
	**Reading Standards for Literacy in History/Social Studies**	
	**Key Ideas and Details**	
RH.6.1	Cite specific textual evidence to support analysis of primary and secondary sources.	14
RH.6.2	Determine the central ideas of information of a primary or secondary source; provide an accurate summary of the source distinct from prior knowledge or opinions.	14
RH.6.3	Identify key steps in a text's description of a process related to history/social studies (e.g., how a bill becomes a law, how interest rates are raised and lowered).	10
	**Craft and Structure**	
RH.6.4	Determine the meaning of words and phrases as they are used in a text, including vocabulary specific to domains related to history/social studies.	11
RH.6.5	Describe how a text presents information (e.g., sequentially, comparatively, causally).	9
RH.6.6	Identify aspects of a text that reveal an author's point of view or purpose (e.g., loaded language, inclusion or avoidance of particular facts).	13
	**Integration of Knowledge and Ideas**	
RH.6.7	Integrate visual information (e.g., in charts, graphs, photographs, videos, or maps) with other information in print and digital texts.	12
RH.6.8	Distinguish among fact, opinion, and reasoned judgment in a text.	13
RH.6.9	Analyze the relationship between a primary and secondary source on the same topic.	14

Common Core State Standard	Grade 6	Crosswalk Coach Lesson(s)
	**Reading Standards for Literacy in History/Social Studies** *(continued)*	
	**Range of Reading and Level of Text Complexity**	
RH.6.10	By the end of grade 8, read and comprehend history/social studies texts in the grades 6–8 text complexity band independently and proficiently.	8–14
	**Reading Standards for Literacy in Science and Technical Subjects**	
	**Key Ideas and Details**	
RST.6.1	Cite specific textual evidence to support analysis of science and technical texts.	11
RST.6.2	Determine the central ideas or conclusions of a text; provide an accurate summary of the text distinct from prior knowledge or opinions.	11
RST.6.3	Follow precisely a multistep procedure when carrying out experiments, taking measurements, or performing technical tasks.	10
	**Craft and Structure**	
RST.6.4	Determine the meaning of symbols, key terms, and other domain-specific words and phrases as they are used in a specific scientific or technical context relevant to *grades 6–8 texts and topics*.	11
RST.6.5	Analyze the structure an author uses to organize a text, including how the major sections contribute to the whole and to an understanding of the topic.	11
RST.6.6	Analyze the author's purpose in providing an explanation, describing a procedure, or discussing an experiment in a text.	11
	**Integration of Knowledge and Ideas**	
RST.6.7	Integrate quantitative or technical information expressed in words in a text with a version of that information expressed visually (e.g., in a flowchart, diagram, model, graph, or table).	12
RST.6.8	Distinguish among facts, reasoned judgment based on research findings, and speculation in a text.	13
RST.6.9	Compare and contrast the information gained from experiments, simulations, video, or multimedia sources with that gained from reading a text on the same topic.	14
	**Range of Reading and Level of Text Complexity**	
RST.6.10	By the end of grade 8, read and comprehend science/technical texts in the grades 6–8 text complexity band independently and proficiently.	8–14
	**Writing Standards for Literacy in History/Social Studies, Science, and Technical Subjects**	
	**Text Types and Purposes**	
WHST.6.1	Write arguments focused on *discipline-specific content*. a. Introduce claim(s) about a topic or issue, acknowledge and distinguish the claim(s) from alternate or opposing claims, and organize the reasons and evidence logically. b. Support claim(s) with logical reasoning and relevant, accurate data and evidence that demonstrate an understanding of the topic or text, using credible sources. c. Use words, phrases, and clauses to create cohesion and clarify the relationships among claim(s), counterclaims, reasons, and evidence. d. Establish and maintain a formal style. e. Provide a concluding statement or section that follows from and supports the argument presented.	15

Common Core State Standard	Grade 6	Crosswalk Coach Lesson(s)
	**Writing Standards for Literacy in History/Social Studies, Science, and Technical Subjects** *(continued)*	
	**Text Types and Purposes** *(continued)*	
WHST.6.2	Write informative/explanatory texts, including the narration of historical events, scientific procedures/experiments, or technical processes. a. Introduce a topic clearly, previewing what is to follow; organize ideas, concepts, and information into broader categories as appropriate to achieving purpose; include formatting (e.g., headings), graphics (e.g., charts, tables), and multimedia when useful to aiding comprehension. b. Develop the topic with relevant, well-chosen facts, definitions, concrete details, quotations, or other information and examples. c. Use appropriate and varied transitions to create cohesion and clarify the relationships among ideas and concepts. d. Use precise language and domain-specific vocabulary to inform about or explain the topic. e. Establish and maintain a formal style and objective tone. f. Provide a concluding statement or section that follows from and supports the information or explanation presented.	16
	**Production and Distribution of Writing**	
WHST.6.4	Produce clear and coherent writing in which the development, organization, and style are appropriate to task, purpose, and audience.	18
WHST.6.5	With some guidance and support from peers and adults, develop and strengthen writing as needed by planning, revising, editing, rewriting, or trying a new approach, focusing on how well purpose and audience have been addressed.	18
WHST.6.6	Use technology, including the Internet, to produce and publish writing and present the relationships between information and ideas clearly and efficiently.	18
	**Research to Build and Present Knowledge**	
WHST.6.7	Conduct short research projects to answer a question (including a self-generated question), drawing on several sources and generating additional related, focused questions that allow for multiple avenues of exploration.	19
WHST.6.8	Gather relevant information from multiple print and digital sources, using search terms effectively; assess the credibility and accuracy of each source; and quote or paraphrase the data and conclusions of others while avoiding plagiarism and following a standard format for citation.	19
WHST.6.9	Draw evidence from informational texts to support analysis reflection, and research.	14
	**Range of Writing**	
WHST.6.10	Write routinely over extended time frames (time for reflection and revision) and shorter time frames (a single sitting or a day or two) for a range of discipline-specific tasks, purposes, and audiences.	15–17

CHAPTER

1

Literature

Diagnostic Assessment for Lessons 1–7

Read the passage and answer the questions that follow.

"The Man Who Died"

excerpted and adapted from

The Thirty-nine Steps

by John Buchan

I returned from the city about three o'clock on that May afternoon pretty well disgusted with life. I had been three months in the Old Country, and was fed up with it. If anyone had told me a year ago that I would have been feeling like that, I should have laughed at him; but there was the fact. The weather made me irritable, the talk of the ordinary Englishman made me sick, I couldn't get enough exercise, and the amusements of London seemed as flat as soda water that has been standing in the sun. "Richard Hannay," I kept telling myself, "you have got into the wrong ditch, my friend, and you had better climb out."

It made me bite my lips to think of the plans I had been building up those last years in Bulawayo. I had got my pile—not one of the big ones, but good enough for me; and I had figured out all kinds of ways of enjoying myself. My father had brought me out from Scotland at the age of six, and I had never been home since; so England was a sort of Arabian Nights to me, and I counted on stopping there for the rest of my days.

But from the first I was disappointed with it. In about a week I was tired of seeing sights, and in less than a month I had had enough of restaurants and theaters and racetracks. I had no real pal to go about with, which probably explains things. Plenty of people invited me to their houses, but they didn't seem much interested in me. They would fling me a question or two about South Africa, and then get on their own affairs. A lot of Imperialist ladies asked me to tea to meet schoolmasters from New Zealand and editors from Vancouver, and that was the most dismal business of all. Here was I, thirty-seven years old, sound in wind and limb, with enough money to have a good time, yawning my head off all day. I had just about settled to clear out and get back to the veldt, the open grazing area of South Africa, for I was the best bored man in the United Kingdom.

About six o'clock I went home, dressed, dined at the Café Royal, and turned into a music hall. It was a silly show, and I did not stay long. The night was fine and clear as I walked back to the apartment I had rented near Portland Place. The crowd surged past me on the pavements, busy and chattering, and I envied the people for having something to do. These shop girls and clerks and dandies and policemen had some interest in life that kept them going. I gave half a crown to a beggar because I saw him yawn; he was a fellow sufferer. At Oxford Circus I looked up into the spring sky, and I made a vow. I would give the Old Country another day to fit me into something; if nothing happened, I would take the next boat for the Cape.

My flat was the first floor in a new block behind Langham Place. There was a common staircase, with a porter and a liftman at the entrance, but there was no restaurant or anything of that sort, and each flat was quite shut off from the others. I hate servants on the premises, so I had a fellow to look after me who came in by the day. He arrived before eight o'clock every morning and used to depart at seven, for I never dined at home.

I was just fitting my key into the door when I noticed a man at my elbow. I had not seen him approach, and the sudden appearance made me start. He was a slim man, with a short brown beard and small, piercing blue eyes. I recognized him as the occupant of a flat on the top floor, with whom I had passed the time of day on the stairs.

"Can I speak to you?" he said. "May I come in for a minute?" He was steadying his voice with an effort, and his hand was pawing my arm.

I got my door open and motioned him in. No sooner was he over the threshold that he made a dash for my back room, where I used to smoke and write my letters. Then he bolted back.

"Is the door locked?" he asked feverishly, and he fastened the chain with his own hand. "I am very sorry," he said humbly. "It's a mighty liberty, but you look the kind of man who would understand. I've had you in my mind all this week when things got troublesome. Say, will you do me a good turn?"

"I'll listen to you," I said. "That's all I'll promise." I was getting worried by the antics of this nervous little chap.

"Pardon," he said, "I'm a bit rattled tonight. You see, I happen at this moment to be dead."

1. Which word BEST describes the main character, Richard Hannay?

   A. daring

   B. bored

   C. frightened

   D. excitable

2. Which event in the story is the rising action?

   A. Richard sees the sights of London.

   B. Richard goes out to dinner.

   C. Richard goes to the theater.

   D. Richard runs into one of his neighbors.

3. What is the theme of the passage?

   A. Always be prepared.

   B. Better safe than sorry.

   C. Life can have some unexpected moments.

   D. People are not as nice as you would expect.

4. From which point of view is the passage written?

   A. first person

   B. second person

   C. third-person limited

   D. third-person omniscient

5. Read the following sentence from the passage.

   If anyone had told me a year ago that I would have been feeling like that, I should have laughed at him.

   What does the literary device in the sentence do?

   A. foreshadows what may happen later in the passage

   B. flashes back to an earlier time before the passage's events

   C. personifies laughter by giving it human emotions

   D. uses a metaphor to compare the narrator's feelings to a year

Read the passage and answer the questions that follow.

"Chapter 1: Loomings"

excerpted and adapted from

Moby-Dick

by Herman Melville

Call me Ishmael. Some years ago—never mind how long precisely—having little or no money in my purse, and nothing particular to interest me on shore, I thought I would sail about a little and see the watery part of the world. I get this feeling any time I am feeling down. Whenever it is a damp, drizzly November in my soul; whenever I find myself pausing before coffin warehouses, and bringing up the rear of every funeral I meet, I think of going to the sea. At times like this, it requires a strong moral principle to prevent me from deliberately stepping into the street, and methodically knocking people's hats off—then, I account it high time to get to sea as soon as I can. This is my substitute for pistol and ball. Yes, instead of death, I quietly choose to take to the ship. There is nothing surprising in this. If they but knew it, almost all men in their degree, some time or other, cherish very nearly the same feelings toward the ocean as I do.

There now is your narrow-minded city of the Manhattoes, belted round by wharves as Indian isles by coral reefs—commerce surrounds it with her surf. Right and left, the streets take you toward the seas. Its extreme downtown is the battery, where that noble mole is washed by waves, and cooled by breezes, which a few hours previous were out of sight of land. Look at the crowds of water gazers there.

Walk all the way around the city of a dreamy Sunday afternoon. Go from Corlears Hook to Coenties Slip, and from there, go north toward Whitehall. What do you see? Like silent soldiers all around the town, stand thousands upon thousands of mortal men fixed in their dreams of the sea. Some leaning against equipment; some seated upon barrels; some looking over the walls of ships from China; some high up in the sails, as if striving to get a still better view of the sea. But these are all landsmen; spending their weekdays laboring, tied to counters, nailed to benches, clinched to desks. How then is this? Are the green fields gone? Why do they come to the sea?

But look! Here come more crowds, pacing straight for the water, and ready to dive right in. Strange! Nothing will make them happy except the most extreme limit of the land. It is not enough for them to stand idly under the shady shelter of distant warehouses. No. They must get just as close to the water as they possibly can without falling, and there they stand—miles of them. All of them live off the land. They come from lanes and alleys, streets, avenues—north, east, south, and west. Yet here they all unite. Tell me, does the magnetism of the compass needles of all those ships attract them there?

Once more. Say you are in the country; in some high land of lakes. Take almost any path you please, and ten to one it carries you down in a valley, and leaves you there by a pool in the stream. There is magic in it. Let the most absent-minded of men be plunged in his deepest daydreams. Yet stand that man on his legs, set his feet a-going, and he will never fail to lead you to water, if any water exists in all of that region.

Now, when I say that I am in the habit of going to sea whenever I am feeling down and out, I do not mean to make you think that I would ever go to sea as a passenger. For to go as a passenger you must have a purse. And a purse is but a rag unless you have money in it. Besides, passengers get seasick, they grow quarrelsome, they don't sleep well in the ocean nights. They just do not enjoy themselves much, as a general thing. No, I never go as a passenger. And even though I am something of an experienced sailor, I never go to sea as an officer, or a captain, or a cook. I abandon the glory and distinction of such offices to those who like them. For my part, I detest all honorable, respectable labors of every kind whatsoever. It is quite enough to simply take care of myself, without worrying about taking care of ships, brigs, schooners, and what not. And as for going as cook, I do confess there is considerable glory in that. Yet, somehow, I never fancied broiling fowls. Though once broiled, sensibly buttered, and perfectly salted and peppered, there is no one who will speak more respectfully of a broiled fowl than I will. Even the old Egyptians worshiped their broiled birds and roasted river horses so much that they mummified those old creatures in their huge bake houses in the pyramids. But no, I do not go to sea as a cook.

6. What can you infer about Ishmael?

    A. He is a tough and opinionated person.

    B. He is a gentle person and eager to please others.

    C. He is a talented farmer and laborer on land.

    D. He dislikes other people who go to the sea.

7. Read the following sentence from the passage.

    And a purse is but a rag unless you have money in it.

    What kind of figurative language is used in the sentence?

    A. personification

    B. foreshadowing

    C. simile

    D. metaphor

8. In paragraph 1, the main character flashes back to earlier times in his life. How does this help the reader to better understand the story?

    A. It tells the reader why he has gone to the sea in the past.

    B. It tells the reader what he can expect to find at sea.

    C. It tells the reader why most other people like to go to the sea.

    D. It gives the reader details about the character's childhood and family.

9. What text evidence does the author give about the story's setting?

    A. There is discussion of current technologies that are used at sea.

    B. There is no current technology, and the narrator talks about living off the land.

    C. The narrator mentions the Egyptians and thcir way of life.

    D. The narrator speculates about what life at sea will be like in the future.

10. How do the topics and themes in the chapters from *The Thirty-nine Steps* and *Moby-Dick* compare and contrast with each other?

_____

_____

_____

_____

_____

_____

_____

_____

1 Character and Plot

RL.6.3, RL.6.10

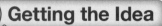

Getting the Idea

Authors use characters and plot to create effective stories. By understanding each of these elements, you can better understand the story and its main ideas.

Character

A **character** is a person, animal, or other creature in a story. The **main character** is the character that the writer focuses on the most. The main character has to solve the central problem in the story.

Characters have **traits**, or qualities, that tell the reader what kind of person they are. A character may be honest, hardworking, shy, or mischievous, for example. When the character deals with the problem of the story, he or she may have to adapt, or change, in order to move toward a resolution. For example, a shy character may have to act bravely in order to solve the problem.

Plot

The **plot** is the sequence of events in a story. The plot of a story is a series of episodes that has a beginning, middle, and end. In the beginning of a story, the author introduces the characters, when and where the story takes place, and the conflict.

A **conflict** is a problem in a story that needs to be solved. It is introduced in the beginning of the story. Some conflicts involve a person versus another person; some involve a character versus himself or herself; and some conflicts involve a character versus nature. The main character and supporting characters are part of the plot and contribute to the conflict, the rising action, the climax, and the resolution.

In the middle of a story, the action rises and the characters try to solve the conflict. Near the end of a story, there is a **climax**, or action that helps the characters resolve the conflict. A **resolution** is the way a conflict is solved at the end.

A good story show how a character changes throughout the plot. If you compare the beginning of the story to the end of the story, you may see how the character has gone through new experiences or has done things that he or she would normally not do.

The following paragraph is a sample story that shows characters and plot.

Jenna stood backstage, going over the notes in her mind. Her flute solo would only be five minutes long, but they would be the most important five minutes of her life. For years, Jenna had been the shyest student in the school. She sat in the back of every class and never volunteered an answer to a question. She found it very painful to make eye contact with people, especially any teacher she had. Then Ms. Diaz had come to Jenna's middle school to teach music. Jenna always loved music, and it was extremely difficult for her to get herself to volunteer and sign up for flute lessons, even though it was something she had always wanted to do. But she signed up, worked hard, and practiced until she became the best flute player in the school. As she slowly gained confidence in her ability to play the flute, she became a more confident person. She knew she could do this solo without a problem. She had practiced more hours than she could even keep track of. "You're on, Jenna," a voice whispered from behind the curtain. Without hesitation, Jenna stepped into the floodlight on stage.

In the paragraph above, Jenna is the main character, and Ms. Diaz is a supporting character. Jenna's main character trait is her shyness, and this also creates a conflict in the story. Jenna wishes she had the courage to take flute lessons when Ms. Diaz comes to the school. In an effort to solve her problem, Jenna does something unexpected of her character. She works hard at learning the flute and ends up performing a solo onstage in front of an audience.

Thinking It Through

Read the following paragraph, and then answer the question that follows.

Max hated sitting in the front of the bus because it always meant the same thing—his little sister Penny would want to sit next to him. Max wanted to show that he was a "big" kid at school now and that he didn't have to sit with little first graders. But today was a stormy and miserable day. Penny had always been afraid of thunder for as long as Max could remember. When the school bus stopped to pick them up that morning, Penny was crying and shaking with fear. *Why does there have to be a thunderstorm on the way to school?* Max thought. But he looked down at Penny and felt bad for her. *I guess being a "big" boy means taking care of the little kids*, he thought. They both got onto the bus together, and he sat right next to her with his arm around her shoulder.

How does Max change in order to resolve his conflict?

_____

_____

_____

_____

HINT   What are Max's thoughts at the beginning and at the end of the paragraph?

Coached Example

Read the passage and answer the questions.

It was Tyrone's first day of work. He sat in his car nervously as the traffic came to a full stop on Main Street. He left his house with enough time to get there ten minutes early, and now it looked as if he would be at least twenty minutes late. There was an accident up ahead, and it looked pretty serious.

Tyrone began to worry about his new job. Would he still have it when he got there so late on his first day? What would his new boss say? He really needed that job to help pay for college. He wished he had a cell phone so that he could call.

1. What details from the story give the reader the idea that Tyrone will be a good employee?

   A. He has a job.

   B. He sits in traffic without getting angry.

   C. He takes a car to work.

   D. He thinks about what his boss will say.

   HINT A character's actions can tell you about his or her traits.

2. Which part of a story's plot is shown in the passage?

   A. conflict

   B. rising action

   C. climax

   D. resolution

   HINT How are parts of a plot divided into the beginning, middle, and end of a story?

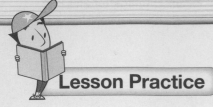

Lesson Practice

Use the Reading Guide to help you understand the passage.

Reading Guide

Which part of the plot are the events in paragraph 2?

What does the reader learn about Dave's personality?

How are Dave's and Rick's characters alike and different?

Mystery of the Missing Breakfast

Dave awoke in his sleeping bag as soon as the first ray of sunshine hit his face. He was excited about camping. He walked to the fire pit to start breakfast before anyone else awoke. Dave was excited about a quiet, peaceful day in the woods.

He didn't get far cooking breakfast, however. The pancake mix was missing! The hot dog rolls and popcorn were gone too!

Dave quietly woke the other campers, still not wanting to break the peaceful silence of the morning. They all gathered around, wondering what had happened to their food. They checked their packs for other missing items, but only the food was missing.

"This puts quite a damper on our peaceful trip," said Dave. He sat on a rock and sulked.

Then they all heard a scampering of leaves just beyond the campsite. "Did you hear that?" asked Rick. He tiptoed toward the sound. The scampering was quiet, and then continued more fiercely.

"Aha!" yelled Rick, pulling back the leaves of a bush. Dave ran to his side and saw the culprits. Two raccoons had dragged their pancake mix, hot dog rolls, and popcorn into the bushes.

"Out! Out! Go on!" screamed Dave in the stillness of the morning. "Shoo! That's ours!"

As the raccoons scampered away, Rick mumbled, "Mystery solved. I'm going back to bed."

Answer the following questions.

1. Who is the main character of the story?

    A. Rick

    B. Dave

    C. the food

    D. the raccoons

2. Which event is the climax of the story?

    A. Dave wakes up his friends.

    B. Rick goes to see what is causing the rustling in the bushes.

    C. Dave scares away the raccoons.

    D. Rick goes back to bed.

3. How did Dave change as the conflict began to be resolved?

    A. He became angry at his friends for not helping.

    B. He decided that he no longer likes camping.

    C. He was no longer concerned with keeping the campsite quiet and peaceful.

    D. He decided to change the breakfast menu that he had worked so hard preparing.

4. Who is the conflict of the story between?

    A. Dave vs. nature

    B. Dave vs. himself

    C. Dave vs. Rick

    D. Dave vs. the other campers

5. What role did Rick play in resolving the conflict of the story?

    _____

    _____

    _____

    _____

    _____

2 Point of View

RL.6.6, RL.6.10

Getting the Idea

A **point of view** is the way a narrator tells a story. A **narrator** is the person who tells the story.

First-person point of view is when a character tells a story using the pronoun *I* or *we*. The story is told by one of the characters in the story. Read this example.

> I looked up and down the aisle at all the packages of rice. Mom will never believe me when I tell her that they are out of her favorite brand!

Third-person point of view is when the narrator tells the story using the pronouns *they, he,* or *she*. There are two kinds of third-person narration.

Third-person omniscient point of view is when the narrator knows everything about the story, including the thoughts, feelings, and actions of all of the characters. Read this example.

> Aaron stared at Evan, wondering why he was being so mean. Evan couldn't believe that Aaron couldn't understand his side of the story.

Third-person limited point of view is when the narrator tells the story through the thoughts and feelings of only one character. Read this example.

> Netavia opened her book with a nervous feeling. The class stared at her. She swallowed hard and began reading aloud.

Second-person point of view uses the pronoun *you*. This point of view is rarely used in stories but is often used in poetry. Below is the first stanza of Robert Browning's "Youth and Art."

> Your trade was with sticks and clay,
> You thumbed, thrust, patted, and polished,
> Then laughed "They will see some day,
> Smith made, and Gibson demolished."

Read the paragraph below. Pay attention to how the narrator tells the story.

> After three days of arguing with her best friend, Aubrey was ready to make up with Layla. As hard as it was for Aubrey to admit it, she thought she was beginning to understand Layla's reason for being angry. Last Friday night, Aubrey was very late picking up Layla for the movies. Aubrey felt anxious and upset about being so late picking up her friend, but it seemed that Layla probably felt even worse. The girls got into a huge argument and didn't speak for days. Aubrey eventually realized that Layla thought she had forgotten about her entirely or was not picking her up to be mean. Aubrey felt sad and lonely without her best friend. She picked up the phone to dial Layla. *Maybe we can work this out*, Aubrey thought.

Think about who is narrating the story. Since there is no *I* or *you* mentioned, it cannot be in the first or second person. This must be written in the third-person point of view. Now think about whether the narrator knows everything about all of the characters, or just one character. The narrator knows about Aubrey's thoughts and feelings, but not Layla's. Even though Aubrey's character thinks about Layla and how she may be feeling, all of the events are told through Aubrey's point of view, and it is Aubrey's opinions that are given. That means the story is told in the third-person limited point of view.

Thinking It Through

Read the following paragraph, and then answer the question that follows.

Greg knocked at the door softly. When it opened, an angry face looked back at him. Greg was frightened, so he muttered an apology and started to leave. "Oh, you're selling candy for school," the man said. Then he smiled and added, "Sorry to be rude. I thought you were someone else. I'd love to buy some!"

From which point of view is the paragraph written? Tell how you know.

_____

_____

_____

_____

HINT Ask yourself whether the narrator is a character in the story. What does the narrator know about the other characters?

Coached Example

Read the poem and answer the questions.

I finally feel alright today—
Yesterday was a tough, tough day.
They say to take each day one at a time—
To me, there is no other way.

If you find yourself like I did,
Feeling blue and really down,
Look to the sky and take a few minutes
Maybe some good feelings will come around.

---

1. This poem is written from which point of view?

   A. first person

   B. second person

   C. third-person limited

   D. third-person omniscient

   HINT Ask yourself whether the narrator is a character in the poem.

2. Which word is the BEST clue about the point of view of the poem?

   A. Yesterday

   B. yourself

   C. I

   D. you

   HINT Think about how the narrator refers to himself or herself.

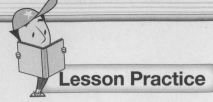

Lesson Practice

Use the Reading Guide to help you understand the passage.

Reading Guide

The word *I* gives a clue about the point of view of the story. However, is the narrator saying the word *I*, or is "I" a character in the story?

Whose feelings is the narrator telling about in the last paragraph?

Do you know each character's thoughts?

A Frog in the Well
a Chinese fable

Once, a frog that lived in a well bragged to a turtle that lived in the sea.

"I am so happy!" cried the frog. "When I go out, I can't wait to return home again and float within the walls of my beloved well. It is the perfect home for any creature, great or small.

"I am lord of this well," the frog continued. "My happiness is great. My dear sir, why don't you come more often and look around my place?"

The turtle from the sea agreed to visit the frog's well. However, before the turtle could get his foot in the well, his right foot got stuck. He hesitated and retreated. The turtle told the frog about his life in the sea.

"Even a distance of a thousand miles cannot give you an idea of the sea's width. And even a height of a thousand feet cannot give you an idea of its depth. The sea is nothing like a well. It does not change along with the passage of time. Its level does not rise or fall according to the amount of rain that falls. The greatest happiness for any creature is to live in the sea."

Hearing these words, the frog of the shallow well suddenly realized his own insignificance and became very ill at ease. He climbed out of the well and crawled off, never to return.

Answer the following questions.

1. From what point of view is the story told?

   A. first person

   B. second person

   C. third-person limited

   D. third-person omniscient

2. The narrator mainly reveals the thoughts and feelings of

   A. the frog.

   B. the turtle.

   C. both characters.

   D. neither character.

3. Why did the turtle tell the frog about his life in the sea?

   A. The frog stopped talking long enough for the turtle to speak.

   B. The frog told the turtle that he is sick of the sea.

   C. The turtle got stuck trying to get into the well after the frog had bragged about it.

   D. The turtle decided that he wanted to dig his own well to live in.

4. At the end of the story, why did the frog never return?

   A. He felt embarrassed about bragging about his well.

   B. He went to build a new well.

   C. He went to live in the sea.

   D. He tried to find a better well to show the turtle.

5. How does the author establish the frog's point of view in the story?

   _____

   _____

   _____

   _____

   _____

3 Theme and Summary

RL.6.2, RL.6.10

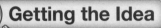

Getting the Idea

A **theme** is a main message or lesson in a text. A theme expresses a general statement that goes beyond the specific events of the text. Many times, a theme is not stated directly in the text. More commonly, the reader must figure out the theme. Some stories have more than one theme.

Here is a list of themes commonly found in literature.

- Be true to yourself.
- Hard work pays off.
- Good triumphs over evil.
- Always do the right thing.

The theme can sometimes be determined from the characters' actions. Read the following story. Try to figure out the theme.

> Jason found the latest action figure at the toy store, but he didn't have enough money to buy it. He was one dollar short. Worst of all, this was the only figure available. He knew that if he left the store, someone else would surely buy it. He needed to come up with a plan. Jason took the figure off the rack and went to the aisle that had the toddler toys. He stashed the figure behind a box of a kid toy and left the store.
>
> A worker noticed what Jason had done and put the action figure back in its proper place. A few minutes later another boy entered the store with his uncle and bought the action figure. When Jason returned later, he was shocked to discover that the toy was not where he had left it! The worker told Jason that he could have asked the clerk at the register to hold the toy until he came back. But since he dishonestly tried to hide the toy, the worker felt it was not fair to anyone else who wanted to buy it.

The theme of the passage could be expressed as *actions have their consequences*.

A **summary** is a short retelling of a text in the reader's own words. A summary should include the main idea and the most important details. It may also include the theme. A summary should not include the reader's opinion or judgments about the passage.

Read the summary below of the story from the previous page. Notice the underlined sentences. These should be removed to make a more efficient summary. The last sentence can also be rewritten to fit in with the rest of the summary.

> Jason is a selfish and dishonest kid. He wanted to buy the last action figure, but he was one dollar short. He hid the action figure so no one else could buy it. But a store employee noticed what Jason had done and returned the toy to its proper place. Another boy bought the toy. The boy came in with his uncle, so the uncle must have had enough money to buy the toy. Jason was foolish for thinking he could stash away the toy and return later. What was he thinking? Doesn't he realize that the employees fix and arrange the shelves all the time? He should also know that actions have their consequences.

The underlined sentences include the reader's personal opinions and judgments. These do not tell about the main idea or most important details. Also, the underlined sentence "The boy came in with his uncle" is a minor detail.

A better summary would be the following.

> Jason hid an action figure in a store and thought he could return later to buy it. But a store employee replaced the action figure so that another customer could buy it. When Jason returned to the store and discovered that the figure had been sold, he learned that actions have their consequences.

Thinking It Through

Read the following paragraph, and then answer the question that follows.

Luis rolled his wheelchair onto the basketball court for the first time. The rest of the team couldn't believe their eyes. Coach had told them that the new student in school would probably be the team's star and would help them win games all season long. This was Coach's secret weapon? The students wondered how Luis could even get himself across the court, let alone handle making baskets during fast game play. Some of the players sighed in disappointment. *Another year in last place*, they thought. But as soon as the whistle blew and the ball was in play, Luis was the fastest, most skilled, and definitely the most talented player on the court. He managed to keep the ball in play and make three baskets before the end of the first quarter.

What is the theme?

_____

_____

_____

_____

HINT A theme doesn't summarize the events as much as it tells the lesson that the reader might have learned.

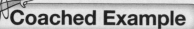

Coached Example

Read the passage and answer the questions.

Cara woke up exhausted on Saturday morning. She had been out with her friends too late the night before and had the time of her life. Why did she agree to work at the soup kitchen over the summer? She should be having fun! She's in the prime of her life. She dragged herself out of bed and got ready for the long day ahead of her.

When she arrived at the soup kitchen, she knew she had done the right thing. There was a family waiting patiently for breakfast, and the little children looked so hungry. She immediately unlocked the door and let them inside.

---

1. Which of the following is the theme of the passage?

   A. Summers are for having fun.

   B. Everyone should have something to do.

   C. Do what your heart wants to do.

   D. Do the right thing.

   HINT Compare how Cara feels with what she does.

2. Which of the following sentences should be part of the passage summary?

   A. Cara had a great time out with her friends.

   B. Cara knew she had made the right decision.

   C. Cara showered and put on her favorite clothes.

   D. Cara should have planned her night better.

   HINT A summary includes only the most important ideas.

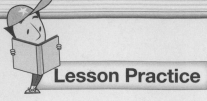

Lesson Practice

Use the Reading Guide to help you understand the passage.

Reading Guide

Based on paragraph 1, what theme might this passage have?

How is the Camel's response to the other animals important to the theme of the passage?

What parts of the passage would you include in a summary?

adapted from
How the Camel Got Its Hump
by Rudyard Kipling

Long ago, there was a Camel. He lived in the middle of a desert because he did not want to work.

One day, the Horse came to him and said, "Camel, come and carry things like the rest of us."

"Humph!" said the Camel.

Soon, the Dog came to him and said, "Camel, come and fetch like the rest of us."

"Humph!" said the Camel.

Then the Ox came to him and said, "Camel, come and plow like the rest of us."

"Humph!" said the Camel.

So the Man told the Horse, Dog, and Ox that they had to work double-time to make up for the Camel. Then, a Genie rolled in on a cloud of dust. The animals complained to him about the Camel's laziness. The Genie agreed that it was wrong for the Camel to do no work while they worked twice as hard.

"My friend," said the Genie to the Camel, "what is this I hear of your doing no work?"

"Humph!" said the Camel.

No sooner had he said it than he saw his back puffing up into a great big humph. "That's your very own humph that you've brought upon yourself," said the Genie. "Now get to work."

From that day the Camel wears a humph, or as we call it now, a hump.

Answer the following questions.

1. Which of the following is the theme of the passage?

    A. There is no justice in this world.

    B. Everyone must do his fair share.

    C. Everyone deserves a second chance.

    D. Complaining never does anyone any good.

2. Which character's actions help determine the theme?

    A. Camel

    B. Genie

    C. Dog

    D. Ox

3. The passage teaches that

    A. actions have their consequences.

    B. a true friend is a friend forever.

    C. power is dangerous in the wrong hands.

    D. there is nothing wrong with being different.

4. Which statement would NOT be appropriate in a summary of the passage?

    A. Camel thought it was okay to be lazy.

    B. Genie taught the Camel a lesson.

    C. I did not like the way the story ended.

    D. Camels have had humps ever since that day.

5. Write a summary of the passage on the lines below.

    _____

    _____

    _____

    _____

    _____

4 Figurative Language

RL.6.4, RL.6.10, L.6.5.a

Getting the Idea

An author can choose to use different language when writing. **Literal language** is language that means exactly what it says.

> There were dozens of bees in the hive.

Figurative language is language that does not mean exactly what it says. Instead, figurative language implies, or suggests, something else. There are several kinds of figurative language. The reader must think about the context of the sentence or paragraph to figure out the meaning of figurative language.

Types of Figurative Language

Figurative Language	Definition	Example	Meaning
idiom	a saying or phrase whose meaning is different from the individual words that make it up	Those hats are a dime a dozen.	Those hats are available anywhere.
metaphor	a comparison that is implied or suggested without using the word *like* or *as*	Jeannie is a fountain of knowledge.	Jeannie knows a lot of information, just as a fountain holds a lot of water.
personification	giving human qualities to an animal, object, or idea	The chair felt sad and lonely when Uncle Joe was not sitting in it.	Uncle Joe sits so much in the chair, they are practically companions.
simile	a direct comparison of one thing to another using the word *like* or *as*	The woman's face looked as wrinkled as an old paper bag.	The woman's face is old and lined with wrinkles.

The following passage uses literal and figurative language. Read it carefully and see if you can find the language that is not meant to be taken literally.

> Carrie's allowance always burned a hole in her pocket. She just had to spend it as fast as she got it. When her mother gave her the money, Carrie ran down to the corner store. She bought a magazine, some juice, and an apple. She had no money left. She thought about her shopping addiction as she walked home. She never seemed to have any money. For Christmas, her grandmother had given her a $50 bill, but she immediately spent the money on clothes. Then she was as poor as a pauper once again. If there was ever any money in Carrie's wallet, it seemed to make her lose her mind.

The passage mainly uses literal language to tell the story, but some figurative language is used to set a tone and affect the meaning. The first sentence of the story is an idiom that helps set a casual tone. The last two sentences help to continue the tone. The simile *poor as a pauper* and the idiom *lose her mind* help to add flavor to the text and stress the casual tone. The reader must use the context of the paragraph to understand which language should be interpreted literally, and which should be interpreted figuratively.

Thinking It Through

Read the following sentence, and then answer the questions that follow.

The snow continued to creep up to my windowsill like an uninvited guest, peeking in, affecting my concentration, and overstaying its welcome.

What kind of figurative language is used in the sentence? How do you know?

_____

_____

_____

_____

HINT Think about the traits the author gives to the snow. How can snow be like an uninvited guest?

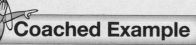

Coached Example

Read the poem and answer the questions.

Some people have <u>hearts of gold</u>
But her heart leaves something to be desired.
No friend or treasure or diamond in the rough,
Thoughtful is not in her vocabulary.

My cat sits on her almighty throne
Looking down on all of us.
Just stay away and leave her be—
Let that chip on her shoulder melt away.

1. What kind of figurative language is used to tell the story in the poem?

    A. idiom

    B. personification

    C. simile

    D. metaphor

    HINT Think about the traits that the author gives to the cat.

2. What is the literal meaning of the phrase <u>hearts of gold</u>?

    A. Some hearts are really made of gold.

    B. Some hearts are worth a lot of money.

    C. Some people are very kind and helpful.

    D. Some people know how to shop for valuable items.

    HINT Use the context of the poem to tell the literal meaning of the idiom.

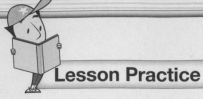

Use the Reading Guide to help you understand the passage.

Reading Guide

Literal language and figurative language are often used in the same stories.

Authors use similes to compare one thing to another.

Which sentences are idioms?

The Family Trip

Every month, Sam's family drove to his grandmother's house in Greensburg. The trip took a few hours, but it seemed more like a million years, and Sam always hated it. The biggest pain in the neck was the music. Dad liked country music, and Mom preferred classical. His brother liked rock, and his sister liked love songs. Sam loved jazz, but he never got to choose which station to play.

If they traveled during the day, they listened to Dad's country music. If it was late, Mom put the classical music on. She wanted to calm everyone down and help them sleep. It didn't work for Sam. Classical music gave him a splitting headache. Sam would have given his right arm for his own personal radio.

Then one night as they were driving home, Sam had enough. "Dad, can we listen to some Wynton Marsalis for a while?" he asked.

"Sure, sport," his father replied to Sam's surprise. Soon the soft sound of a saxophone filled the car. The saxophone whispered in a calm voice for everyone to pay attention.

"It's very peaceful," his mother said. "I like it."

The next time they all rode in the car together, they listened to the mellow tones of jazz. Sam was as happy as a clam.

Answer the following questions.

1. Which sentence from the passage is an example of personification?

   A. "Every month, Sam's family drove to his grandmother's house in Greensburg."

   B. "Classical music gave him a splitting headache."

   C. "The saxophone whispered in a calm voice for everyone to pay attention."

   D. "Sam loved jazz, but he never got to choose which station to play."

2. In paragraph 6, what does the narrator mean when he says that "Sam was as happy as a clam"?

   A. Sam was excited to eat seafood.

   B. Sam enjoyed eating clams.

   C. Sam was very unhappy.

   D. Sam was very happy.

3. In paragraph 2, what does the narrator mean by "Sam would have given his right arm" for his own personal radio?

   A. Sam wished he could trade his arm for a radio.

   B. Sam wished his arm would turn into a radio.

   C. Sam did not really want a radio.

   D. Sam really wanted his own radio.

4. Which of the following phrases from the passage is an idiom?

   A. "She wanted to calm everyone down."

   B. "The biggest pain in the neck was the music."

   C. "Sam loved jazz, but he never got to choose which station to play."

   D. "It didn't work for Sam."

5. Why do you think the author uses literal language along with figurative language to tell about the family car ride?

   _____

   _____

   _____

   _____

   _____

5 Literary Text Structures

RL.6.5, RL.6.10

Getting the Idea

There are different kinds of literature, and each kind is organized in its own special way. A **text structure** is the way an author chooses to present information. A text's structure helps tell the setting of a story. The **setting** of a story is the time and place that a story occurs.

One kind of literature is a story or book. A **book** is a long story written in sentences and paragraphs. The text structure of a book is often organized by chapters. A **chapter** is a division of a book into logical parts. Chapters can be numbered and have names to tell what they are about. Each chapter may have a different setting or purpose within the text of the book. The chapters build on each other to help tell the story and connect with each other to help express the theme. For example, here are some chapter titles from Louisa May Alcott's book *Little Women*.

> Chapter Three: The Laurence Boy
> Chapter Four: Burdens
> Chapter Five: Being Neighborly

Another kind of literature is poetry. **Poetry** is literature written in lines with creative language and often includes rhythm and rhyme. The structure of a poem is organized by stanza. A **stanza** is a group of lines that make up a verse, or one unit of a poem. Each stanza helps contribute to the theme of the poem.

The following are two stanzas from Lewis Carroll's "The Hunting of the Snark."

> "Just the place for a Snark!" the Bellman cried,
> As he landed his crew with care;
> Supporting each man on the top of the tide
> By a finger entwined in his hair.

> "Just the place for a Snark! I have said it twice:
> That alone should encourage the crew.
> Just the place for a Snark! I have said it thrice:
> What I tell you three times is true."

Another kind of literature is a play or drama. **Drama** is literature that is meant to be acted out. Whereas books are divided into chapters, plays are divided into scenes. A **scene** is a part of a play with a particular setting. Each scene leads to the next, and they build on each other to tell the plot just as the chapters of a book would. Each scene takes place in a different setting with a different interaction among characters. A play may have the following scenes.

Scene One: Waiting on the Front Porch
Scene Two: Opening the Special Package

Within a text's structure, an author may use literary devices to help tell the story or express ideas. A **literary device** is a technique used to produce a specific effect on a reader. Literary devices can help tell a story in an interesting way.

One kind of literary device is a flashback. A **flashback** is when there is a pause in a story to describe an earlier event. Flashbacks give the reader additional information about a story or character.

Another device is foreshadowing. **Foreshadowing** is a clue about what is going to happen later in a story. For example, a character on his way to explore a famous cave reads a newspaper article about strange events that have happened in that cave in recent months. Later in the story, the character has a scary experience in the cave. By having the character read the article earlier, the author foreshadowed what was to happen later.

Read the following paragraph and look for literary devices.

Joanne listened to the roar of the wind and the beating of the rain against the windows. The rainstorm had knocked out the power just as Joanne was about to eat dinner. The food sat on the table as Joanne stumbled around the house, lighting candles and closing windows. Last week her cousin Ben had asked her to housesit for him while he went on vacation. "It's a great country house, Joanne. Peaceful, remote, and there's a fireplace. One time the power went out, but only for a couple of hours," Ben had told her. It sounded great to her at the time, but right now Joanne wished she were back in her city apartment.

In the paragraph, the character flashes back to the time when she had looked forward to the trip. The flashback of her conversation with her cousin also foreshadowed the current situation—Ben had once mentioned that the power went out at the house. This helps to add depth to the story. It allows the reader to identify with the character's mixed feelings about the setting and the situation she is in.

Thinking It Through

Read the following passage, and then answer the question that follows.

We entered Aunt Rachel's restaurant through the back kitchen entrance because we knew exactly what she would say if she saw us come through the main door during the lunch rush. Last week she had told Heather and me that seeing noisy teenagers walk through the front door would scare away the business crowd that was searching for a quiet, adult atmosphere. It was really easy to put Aunt Rachel into a bad mood while she was serving the lunch crowd.

"Ah! My favorite niece and nephew are here," Aunt Rachel yelled from the kitchen as she saw us come through the back door. "How would you like some pizza this afternoon?" I looked at Heather and winked.

How does the flashback in paragraph 1 help to set the tone of the scene?

_____

_____

_____

_____

HINT Think about what is being said in the flashback and how that affects the character's actions.

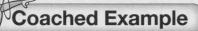

Coached Example

Read the passage and answer the questions.

Rick drank thirstily from his water bottle again. He could hear Liz breathing heavily behind him. He knew she was exhausted and angry about the climb. He thought of their drive up to the woods. "Don't worry, Liz," he'd said. "It's an easy climb. You'll love it." Now Rick wished he hadn't said that. Suddenly, a soft breeze blew through the trees, and the leaves flickered in the sunlight. A bluebird chirped with a song from its nest. Rick smiled, the pack on his back feeling lighter. Liz turned to him, also with a hopeful look on her face. "Just a little longer," he said.

1. Which line from the passage is a flashback?

    A. "Rick drank thirstily from his water bottle again."

    B. "He thought of their drive up to the woods."

    C. "Now Rick wished he hadn't said that."

    D. "Rick smiled, the pack on his back feeling lighter."

    HINT A flashback is a pause in a story to talk about an earlier event.

2. Based on the details at the end of the passage, what do you think the author is trying to foreshadow?

    A. The trip will get harder.

    B. Rick and Liz will be too tired to finish their climb.

    C. The climb will become easier.

    D. It will begin to rain.

    HINT Foreshadowing tells what is going to happen in a story and contributes to the theme.

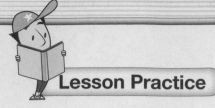

Lesson Practice

Use the Reading Guide to help you understand the passage.

Reading Guide

What is the text structure for this passage?

Look for references to the past or the future.

Think about how a scene change affects the setting of the passage.

Rain on a Parade

Scene 1

Inside Margo and Leena's house.

MARGO: Do you hear that noise from the center of town? It must be the Memorial Day parade getting ready to start. Let's go find a good place to watch it.

LEENA: Are you kidding? Mom said that storms are expected this afternoon. I don't think we should risk it to go look at a silly parade.

MARGO: You're always so cautious. Why don't you take some chances? Our town has only one parade every year. Don't you want to see it?

Scene 2

Sidelines of Memorial Day parade.

LEENA: You're right, Margo. This is a lot of fun! I love to watch a parade, and this one is so close to our house!

(loud clap of thunder)

PARADE ANNOUNCER: Sorry to disappoint you, folks, but we'd better pack it up. There's a big storm headed our way!

(pouring rain and thunderstorm)

MARGO: Yeah, it's a good thing we're so close to home! Run!

Answer the following questions.

1. Read the following lines by Leena.

    Are you kidding? Mom said that storms are expected this afternoon. I don't think we should risk it to go look at a silly parade.

    What kind of literary device is being used?

    A. scene

    B. stanza

    C. foreshadowing

    D. flashback

2. What is the setting of scene 1?

    A. at a parade

    B. in a house

    C. in a storm

    D. at a store

3. What is the importance of the parade announcer?

    A. He cancels the parade.

    B. He foreshadows an important event.

    C. He has a flashback.

    D. He yells at Leena and Margo.

4. Why is the setting important?

    A. It tells where the characters are.

    B. It tells what the characters are like.

    C. It tells the theme of the play.

    D. It tells what each scene is about.

5. Write a new scene in which one of the characters has a flashback.

    _____

    _____

    _____

    _____

    _____

    _____

    _____

    _____

    _____

    _____

6 Comparing and Contrasting Stories

RL.6.9, RL.6.10, W.6.9

Getting the Idea

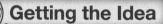

When you **compare** two passages or texts, you tell how they are alike. When you **contrast** two passages or texts, you tell how they are different. Comparing and contrasting information in stories, poems, and articles can help you better understand what you read. You can compare and contrast elements of the same passage, such as the different ways two characters reacted to the same situation. Or you can compare and contrast elements of different passages, such as the topics covered. You can also compare and contrast theme, characters, settings, and genre.

For example, the story of Pinocchio is similar in some ways to the story of Cinderella. Both main characters want to escape from their real worlds and be someone they are not. Both get a little help from magical characters to change their lives for just a little while.

A **genre** is a kind of writing. Some genres of fiction include adventure, mystery, historical narrative, and fantasy. An **adventure story** has a plot with a lot of action in which the characters go on a journey. A **mystery** has a plot in which a puzzle, riddle, or crime must be solved. A **historical narrative** is a made-up story set in a real time in the past and includes characterizations of real people. A **fantasy** includes many elements that could not happen in real life and occur in places that may not exist.

Sometimes, stories in different genres can be compared if they are about similar things. For example, a mystery about a missing dog might be compared to an adventure story about a dog journeying through the state to return home to its owner. The stories are examples of different genres, but they may have similarities that connect them.

Even different kinds of literature, like fiction and poetry, can be compared and contrasted. Read the following examples.

A Farmer's Thoughts

The meadow grass blows;
My horse and buggy halts;
I take a view of the fields
On the wide-open prairie.
This country is new—
May it give us what we need.
The land is our provider.

Lending a Hand to Our Land

Jake can't wait to use his new crop irrigation system. He bought it from a farmer's supply store in the city, and many farmers gave it rave reviews. Jake has begun to rely on these modern technologies to keep his business afloat. Relying on the earth to provide us with our riches can be a risky endeavor. A little technology can go a long way down on the farm!

The two passages can be compared by their theme. They are both about farmers and living off the land. However, the genre of the first passage is a poem, and the genre of the second passage is a story. The poem is set in the past, while the story is set in modern times.

When you compare and contrast literature, you can see how two seemingly different things actually have a lot in common. You can also see how two things that seem similar at first can have many differences between them.

Thinking It Through

Read the following paragraph, and then answer the questions that follow.

   Bill and Sue are pen pals. They write letters to one another, telling each other what is happening in their lives. Bill lives in Tempe, Arizona, near the university. Sue lives in Topeka, Kansas, in the middle of the country. Bill's parents own a hotel, and Sue's parents are farmers. Sue likes the countryside because she can ride horses and go camping. Bill likes his town because there are many places to go skateboarding.

In what ways are Sue's and Bill's interests similar? In what ways are they different?

_____

_____

_____

_____

HINT   Make a list, in your mind or on paper, and look for a pattern.

Coached Example

Read the passages and answer the questions.

The Longest Year

We know that a typical year lasts approximately 365 days. But did you know that there was once a year that lasted for 445 days? It was the year 46 B.C.E, and Julius Caesar, born into an impoverished and little-known family, had become the leader of the Roman Empire. He was upset that the calendar was so out of line with the seasons that spring did not come until May of that year!

Caesar instructed a prominent astronomer to develop a new calendar. The calendar that they had been using had only 355 days, so it was about ten days off the solar year. The solar year is how long it takes Earth to go around the sun one time. In order to have a new calendar that would be in line with the solar year, the calendar year had to be longer. So Caesar simply decreed that there would be two extra months between November and December that year!

Why February Has Twenty-eight Days

Thirty days hath September
April, June, and November;
All the rest have thirty-one,
Save February, with twenty-eight days clear,
And twenty-nine each leap year.

This poem helps people remember how many days are in each month. There's some interesting history about the reasons that different months have different numbers of days. Back during the time of the Roman Empire, Julius Caesar's original calendar showed February having twenty-nine days, so what happened to that extra day? Caesar's adopted son Augustus, the offspring of a wealthy and prominent political couple, stole it.

When Augustus became emperor, the name of a month was changed to "August" in his honor. He felt honored until he realized that his month had thirty days, while July (the month named for Julius Caesar) had thirty-one days. Augustus became furious, and he took a day from February and added it to his month. This made August thirty-one days long and February only twenty-eight days long every three out of four years.

1. What information is described in BOTH passages?

    A. how many months are in a year

    B. where the names of all the twelve months came from

    C. how the calendar has changed

    D. why there are 365 days in a year

    HINT Use your own words to summarize each passage in your head.

2. What kind of historical information do BOTH passages share?

    A. information about the reign of Augustus Caesar

    B. information about the decisions of Julius Caesar

    C. information about important changes in the Roman Empire

    D. information about the work of ancient astronomers

    HINT What historical information or names are in both passages?

3. In what ways do the two passages differ?

    _____

    _____

    _____

    _____

    _____

    HINT Think about ways that the structure of the passages differ as well as ways the content is different.

Lesson Practice

Use the Reading Guides to help you understand the passages.

Reading Guide

Think about who the characters are and what they are experiencing.

What kind of story is this?

Does this story include real people from history?

The Missing Butterfly

Whenever Jonah's teacher was out sick, it meant trouble for whatever substitute was chosen to take over the class. Today was no exception. As soon as the substitute closed the classroom door to start the class, Lori Beth screamed a rather shrill screech.

Everyone turned to look at her. She pointed to the caterpillar cage that had been in the classroom for weeks. The students had watched as the egg grew into a caterpillar, which ate its way through a bunch of leaves, and then went through its pupa stage, all while hanging from one of the branches inside the cage. The class named the caterpillar Sally, and the whole class was attached to her. Now that Sally was a beautiful butterfly, everyone was in love with her. Now the cage door was open and Sally was gone.

Jonah's heart sank. What could have happened to Sally? Would she be safe wherever she is? Then, like the rest of the students, Jonah set his sights on solving this awful crime. Could it be Lori Beth, who first "noticed" that the cage was open?

Then the substitute teacher clapped her hands loudly. "Quiet down!" she said with a raised voice.

"Your beloved Sally is safe here in a jar until class is over," she said. "I hear that she is a major distraction in this classroom, and your attention should be with *me*." She opened a cabinet at the front of the class, and there was Sally, safe and sound atop a leaf inside the jar. Jonah sighed with relief and Lori Beth nearly fell over in disbelief.

Jonah's Class Trip

Jonah's class was the first off the buses at the amusement park. *This is going to be the best class trip in the world*, Jonah thought. Just like everyone else in his class, he was ready for a day of fun. Everyone had their lunches and drinks sitting in their backpacks, and the air around them smelled like sunscreen and bug spray. Even though they knew they would be spending half their time standing in lines to get onto rides, the students were raring to go.

Jonah and Lori Beth were the first in line for the Upside Down Roller Coaster Adventure. Not only did the ride loop upside down, but half the time it went backward and flew around sharp turns. People said that this ride was the scariest in the surrounding four counties. As the two friends waited in line, they both had pits in their stomachs, and the hair on the back of their necks stood up.

But they wouldn't have given up going on the ride for anything. For Jonah, there was something about the excitement of a roller coaster that existed nowhere else in the world.

Lori Beth must have felt the same. When it came time for them to get into the roller coaster car, she grabbed Jonah's hand and yelled his name. "Come on, Jonah!" she screamed. "It's our turn!"

Jonah rode that coaster three times during the course of the day, ate two hot dogs, and had a great time with his friends. It was a day to remember.

On the way back to school in the buses, the atmosphere was happy and content, but deadly quiet. Most students were fast asleep in their seats.

Answer the following questions.

1. What does "The Missing Butterfly" have in common with "Jonah's Class Trip"?

   A. the theme

   B. the genre

   C. the characters

   D. the setting

2. How do the stories differ?

   A. The first is a mystery, and the second is an adventure.

   B. The first is a mystery, and the second is a fantasy.

   C. The first is a historical narrative, and the second is a mystery.

   D. The first is an adventure, and the second is a historical narrative.

3. What can the reader tell about Lori Beth's character from reading both stories?

   A. She likes roller coasters.

   B. She is easily excited.

   C. She enjoys school.

   D. She likes butterflies.

4. Who is the main character of each story?

   A. Lori Beth

   B. Jonah

   C. the substitute teacher

   D. Sally

5. How do the themes of the stories differ from each other?

   _____

   _____

   _____

   _____

   _____

7 Make Inferences

RL.6.1, RL.6.10, RI.6.1

Getting the Idea

An **inference** is an educated guess based on evidence in the text and a reader's prior knowledge. A good inference makes sense and is backed up by details in the passage. When you make inferences as you read, you can get a richer experience and understand the message, theme, or story better. This is often referred to as "reading between the lines."

When you make an inference, you should be able to find evidence in the text that supports what you think. For example, you might read about a character who carries an umbrella and has a frown. Although it is not directly stated, you can infer that it is raining outside, using the umbrella as evidence. You also know from your own experience that you carry an umbrella when it rains. You can also infer that the character is sad, using her frown as evidence. You may go one step further and infer that the rain has made the character sad.

Most often, you will make an inference about how a character feels, and what makes the character feel that way. You may also make an inference about a character's traits based on his or her actions. If you read about a character who cheats on his tests, copies his friend's homework, and pretends to be sick to get out of class, you may infer that he is lazy and dishonest. The author may not use these actual words in the passage, but when you are asked to make an inference about the character, you can use these actions as evidence.

You can also make an inference about a character's actions. For example, the character mentioned in the previous paragraph may have a reason for being lazy and dishonest. You may infer that he does not suffer any consequence for his actions.

The following paragraph does not directly say where Geoff is. Based on your prior knowledge and experience, make an inference about Geoff's surroundings as you read.

> Geoff tenderly touched his left cheek and groaned. He wondered how long it would be before someone called his name. This is what he got for skipping those after-dinner brushings. Suddenly, he heard a cry from behind a door. Geoff shifted in his seat and touched his cheek again. If ever a place needed soundproof walls, this was it.

The author does not directly state that Geoff has a toothache and is waiting at the dentist's office, but you can infer it. The fact that the author does not state directly that Geoff is in a dentist's office helps to add to the setting of the story. Descriptions of the mood, the room, and the scene all help the reader get more information than simply saying that Geoff is at the dentist's office.

The paragraph provides important clues that help the reader make an inference: Geoff feels pain when he touches his cheek, and he regrets not brushing after dinner. He is also waiting for someone to call his name, and he hears someone cry out.

Thinking It Through

Read the following passage, and then answer the question that follows.

Stephen looked up at the deserted house and tried to imagine that he never took the dare in the first place. Now, with his friends Octavio and Will standing next to him, there was no turning back.

"Go on, buddy," Will said with a broad grin. Octavio patted Stephen on the back. "Yeah, what are you waiting for?" Octavio and Will gave each other a glance. Will added, "Hey, don't worry. If you back out, we won't think you're a chicken or anything."

Last week, accepting the dare to spend fifteen minutes in the house had seemed a lot less threatening. Now he felt like a character in a bad movie. Just then a police car pulled up in front of the house. "I hope you boys are not thinking of going in there," he said sternly. "This house is abandoned for a reason. The roof is about to fall in. Please leave the property and go home." The three boys ran away—just in case the roof decided to collapse at that moment.

Based on paragraph 1, what inference can you make about Stephen?

_____

_____

_____

_____

HINT Use text evidence. Stephen wishes he had not taken a dare, but he can't turn back now.

Coached Example

Read the passage and answer the questions.

As Anju awoke, she quickly flipped back her bed sheets. She quietly crept out into the hallway and headed down to the kitchen. There was just one piece of chocolate cake left. She lifted the dome cover off the platter and stared at the sweet confection with growing anticipation. Opening a drawer beneath the counter, Anju silently took a fork, sliced off a piece, and lifted the fork to her mouth. As the chocolate frosting melted in her mouth, Anju closed her eyes. A voice suddenly pierced the silence. "Hey!" Anju dropped the fork and looked up guiltily at her older brother.

1. The reader can infer that

   A. Anju's parents had saved that piece of cake for her.

   B. Anju celebrated her birthday on the previous day.

   C. Anju does not want anyone to know what she is doing.

   D. Anju has never eaten chocolate cake before.

 The correct answer is the one best supported by the passage and Anju's actions.

2. How does Anju's brother MOST LIKELY feel when he sees her eating the cake?

   A. amused

   B. angry

   C. confused

   D. pleased

 The correct answer is supported by the last three sentences in the passage.

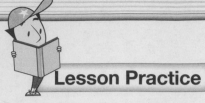

Lesson Practice

Use the Reading Guide to help you understand the passage.

Reading Guide

What clues tell you when the story takes place?

Use text evidence to support any inferences you make about Jasmine's efforts.

Do the other people feel and think the same things Jasmine does?

Living Through the Bus Boycott

Jasmine walked with her mother down the hot Montgomery, Alabama, streets. Her brow was sweating, and her hair was already dripping with perspiration. She heard that the temperatures would be up over one hundred degrees again this afternoon. The perspiration caused her hand to slip easily from her mother's hand, but she kept a firm grip. People sometimes stared at them, and it made Jasmine feel uncomfortable. But she just faced forward and kept walking proudly.

The bus boycott was something that her family was taking very seriously. Ever since Rosa Parks was arrested for refusing to give up her bus seat to a white man, there had been a feeling of outrage in her town.

Jasmine agreed that it wasn't fair to have laws that prevented blacks and whites from sitting together or sharing the same public places. She agreed with Dr. Martin Luther King Jr. when he helped to launch this bus boycott to bring attention to the problem. Jasmine was just very tired of walking everywhere on these hot summer days. She struggled to not look up at the empty buses that drove by, even though she was tempted to climb aboard and sit down to rest her feet. Her efforts to change the laws in her community had to be more important than her desire to take a rest. She walked on.

Answer the following questions.

1. What can you infer about Jasmine from paragraph 1?

    A. She is making an effort to do something difficult.

    B. She does not like Alabama.

    C. She gets along well with her mother.

    D. She is late for an appointment.

2. How does Jasmine MOST LIKELY feel about being part of the bus boycott?

    A. angry

    B. proud

    C. sad

    D. disappointed

3. Which detail in the passage shows that Jasmine thinks she is doing something important?

    A. She is sweating.

    B. She knows how high the temperature will be.

    C. People stare at her.

    D. She keeps walking.

4. If Jasmine had boarded the bus, her mother would MOST LIKELY feel

    A. proud.

    B. happy.

    C. disappointed.

    D. jealous.

5. How do you think Jasmine feels about Rosa Parks?

    _____

    _____

    _____

    _____

Cumulative Assessment for Lessons 1–7

Read the passage and answer the questions that follow.

excerpted from

A Man of the People:
A Drama of Abraham Lincoln
by Thomas Dixon

SCENE II

SET SCENE: *The same as Acts I and II, except that a small table has been placed down center on the side near Lincoln's desk. A telegraph instrument has been installed on this table.*

AT RISE: *The audience sees only* LINCOLN *and* OPERATOR; *the lights gradually rise until full day shows the entire room. It is the morning of September 3, 1864.*

LINCOLN: Now listen! I'm going to tell you something—I *know*! I've a sort of second sight that tells me things sometimes, my dear. After the battle of Gettysburg, I saw General Daniel E. Sickles in the hospital. They told me that he was mortally wounded and could not possibly live. *I* told General Sickles that he *would* live and get well, and he did! I saw his living body that day at work in health and strength as plainly as I see you! We have not heard from Captain Vaughan yet, but it will *come*! He has reached Atlanta. The general got my message. I know that. I felt it flash through the air from his soul to mine! I can see you and your lover at this moment seated side by side smiling and happy.

BETTY: (*in awe*) You see this!

LINCOLN: (*in dreamy tones*) As plainly as I see the sunlight dancing on the leaves outside that window now.

STANTON *enters and* LINCOLN *turns to meet him eagerly.*

STANTON: You've no news?

LINCOLN: I sent for you, to ask that.

STANTON: Nothing.

LINCOLN: (*in low tones*) What does it mean?

STANTON: A storm swept Atlanta yesterday—the wires may be all down.

LINCOLN: You think that's it?

STANTON: No, I don't.

LINCOLN: Neither do I.

STANTON: Something big has happened! Sherman has either taken Atlanta, or Hood has cut his communications, and his army may be imperiled.

LINCOLN: (*his head droops*) That's what I think too!

The sharp click of the telegraph instrument causes him to start quickly, cross to the table, and listen. The committee headed by RAYMOND *and* STEVENS *crowd through the door against the protests of* NICOLAY.

NICOLAY: I promised you an answer in half an hour, gentlemen! You must wait.

RAYMOND: Not another minute!

STEVENS: (*waving a telegram*) The matter is too urgent!

LINCOLN: All right, John. Let them in. I'm ready.

RAYMOND: We have just heard a most painful and startling piece of news from the War Department.

LINCOLN: (*to* STANTON) War Department.

(*low voice*) What is it, Stanton?

STANTON: Something I didn't believe and wouldn't repeat to you.

LINCOLN: (*whispering to* OPERATOR) Pull for me, boy, pull for me. Keep picking at that thing!

STEVENS: (*triumphantly*) You were advised to withhold the new draft of men until after the election! Well, read that copy of a telegram from New York, just received by General Halleck, sir!

Offers telegram to LINCOLN, *and he refuses to take it.*

LINCOLN: I don't want to read it, Stevens. Your face is enough for me. It must be bad, or you wouldn't be so happy. You're almost smiling!

STEVENS: Read it!

LINCOLN: (*ignoring the proffered telegram*) You know, Stevens, you remind me of an old farmer I knew in Illinois.

The committee gathers around LINCOLN *eager for the story, glancing at* STEVENS.

STEVENS: Go on, give them the joke. It's your funeral—not mine!

LINCOLN: (*facing the committee*) This old farmer raised the biggest hog ever seen in the county. He was so fat the news of his size spread over the country, and people came from far and near to see this wonder in pork. A stranger came up one day and asked the farmer to see him. The old man said: "Wal I've got sech a animal an' he's the biggest one I ever seed. I'll say that. But so many folks are comin' here pesterin' me to look at him, I've decided to charge a shillin' a look." The stranger put his hand in his pocket, pulled out the money, paid the shilling, stared at the old man, turned, and walked away. The farmer called after him—"Hi—there—ain't yer goin' ter see the hog?" "No"—the fellow answered—"I've seen you! I've got my money's worth."

All laugh except STEVENS. *During the laugh* LINCOLN *bends over the telegraph instrument—in low tones.*

How goes it, boy? How goes it?

The OPERATOR *shakes his head.*

Not a click?

Operator shakes his head again—and LINCOLN'S *face contracts in suffering.*

STEVENS: Just a minute, Mr. President. I'll give you the telegram if you won't read it.

LINCOLN: Fire away, Stevens, if it makes you happy.

STEVENS: (*reading*) "New York, September 3, 1864.
"The Federal authorities have just discovered a nationwide conspiracy to resist by force of arms the new draft. It will be necessary for General Grant to detach half his army from Lee's front immediately to put down this counter revolution. Send these soldiers without delay to our great cities."
The signature is in code.

1. Which of the following words BEST describes Lincoln's character trait in this passage?

   A. carefree

   B. dangerous

   C. nervous

   D. vengeful

2. What is the plot of the scene?

   A. The president is waiting to hear the results of a battle.

   B. The president is having a good time with his friends.

   C. There are people who want the president to read a telegram.

   D. The president is trying to get reelected.

3. In the flashback, Lincoln recalls

   A. the battle of Gettysburg.

   B. the time he received a telegram from the operator.

   C. the time he saw General Sickles in the hospital.

   D. the last time he talked to the War Department.

4. Where does the scene take place?

   A. during a storm in Atlanta

   B. in Abraham Lincoln's office

   C. during the battle of Gettysburg

   D. in General Lee's office

5. What does the foreshadowing in Lincoln's first piece of dialogue reveal will happen?

   A. Captain Vaughan will never reach Atlanta.

   B. The battle of Gettysburg will soon be over.

   C. General Sickles would be in the hospital again soon.

   D. They will soon receive news from Captain Vaughan.

Read the passage and answer the questions that follow.

President Abraham Lincoln was shot on April 14, 1865. He died the next day from his wounds. Lincoln is the captain referred to in this poem written by Walt Whitman.

O Captain! My Captain!
by Walt Whitman

O CAPTAIN! my Captain! our fearful trip is done,
The ship has weathered every rack, the prize we sought is won,
The port is near, the bells I hear, the people all exulting,
While follow eyes the steady keel, the vessel grim and daring;
5   But O heart! heart! heart!
      O the bleeding drops of red!
       Where on the deck my Captain lies,
        Fallen cold and dead.

O Captain! my Captain! rise up and hear the bells;
10 Rise up—for you the flag is flung—for you the bugle trills,
For you bouquets and ribboned wreaths—for you the shores crowding,
For you they call, the swaying mass, their eager faces turning;
      Here, Captain! dear father!
      This arm beneath your head!
15   It is some dream that on the deck
       You've fallen cold and dead.

My Captain does not answer, his lips are pale and still,
My father does not feel my arm, he has no pulse nor will;
The ship is anchored safe and sound, its voyage closed and done,
20 From fearful trip the victor ship comes in with object won;
      Exult, O shores! and ring, O bells!
       But I, with mournful tread,
        Walk the deck my Captain lies,
         Fallen cold and dead.

6. From what point of view is the poem told?

   A. first person

   B. second person

   C. third-person limited

   D. third-person omniscient

7. What inference can you make about the captain in the poem?

   A. He is not well respected.

   B. He is still fighting in a battle.

   C. He is well respected and loved by the speaker.

   D. He feels that his friends are honorable.

8. What is the theme of the poem?

   A. It is fashionable to give one's life in battle.

   B. It is a disgrace to be injured in battle.

   C. Friends are always nearby.

   D. An honorable leader earns others' respect.

9. Which line from the poem uses personification?

   A. "for you the flag is flung"

   B. "The ship is anchored safe and sound"

   C. "the vessel grim and daring"

   D. "for you they call"

10. How are the theme and topic of "A Man of the People" similar to "O Captain! My Captain!"?

   _____

   _____

   _____

   _____

   _____

CHAPTER

2 Informational Texts

2 Diagnostic Assessment for Lessons 8–14

Read the passage and answer the questions that follow.

Galileo Galilei: A Scientist's Life

Galileo Galilei was born close to five hundred years ago, and we owe some of our everyday knowledge to him. Born in 1564 in Pisa, Italy, Galileo was the oldest of seven children in his family. He studied for years at a monastery, and then he began to study medicine. His education served him well, because Galileo became one of the greatest thinkers of his time. He was curious about things and was always interested in finding the answers to his own questions.

For example, when Galileo was twenty years old, he noticed an overhead lamp swinging in a church. He wanted to know how long it took the lamp to swing back and forth, so he timed the motion with his own pulse. What he discovered was a new and important idea to science. Each swing of the lamp took exactly the same amount of time. Galileo had discovered the "law of the pendulum," which would be used later to regulate the movement of clock pieces. The discovery made him famous.

The law of the pendulum was not the only law of science that Galileo explored. He also tested and disproved one of Aristotle's most popular theories. It was Aristotle who theorized that heavier objects fall faster than lighter objects. Galileo conducted an experiment to prove that all objects fall at the same rate. He carried heavy balls of different sizes and weights to the top of the Tower of Pisa, which was about 177 feet tall. In a big demonstration in front of a crowd of professors and students, he dropped them all off the building and showed that they all landed on the ground at the same time.

To support his family, Galileo tried to come up with scientific inventions that would make him a lot of money. He experimented a bit with magnets, but then settled on constructing his own spyglass that turned out to be the first telescope.

The telescope not only brought him money and additional fame, it also allowed him to make further discoveries about the night sky. His sky-gazing through the telescope enabled him to crush the popular notion that the moon was smooth and polished. Galileo proved that the moon was in fact rough, uneven, and full of craters. The telescope also enabled him to be the first to see some spots next to Jupiter that turned out to be its rings.

In addition to viewing Jupiter's rings, Galileo also used his telescope to notice that small <u>satellites</u> were revolving around Jupiter. This particular discovery caused Galileo to stop and think about the ideas that astronomers had been thinking about for a long time. If objects could orbit Jupiter, then there may be objects that orbit Earth as well. That might mean that Earth is not the center of the universe as people had thought for hundreds of years. It was Nicolaus Copernicus who originally suggested that the sun was the center of the universe, not Earth. People rejected Copernicus's ideas, and his work was considered a failure in his time. Could Galileo's work with telescopes actually prove that Copernicus was correct?

Galileo published his ideas and his findings in 1610 in a book called *The Starry Messenger*. But the book was more than a simple publication of scientific findings. Similar to Copernicus before him, Galileo's ideas were met with a lot of criticism and outrage from the Church. The very idea that Earth was not the center of the universe went against the teachings of the Church. Because Galileo was a religious person himself, he countered that his findings did not go against the Church. He acknowledged that he was not saying the Bible was wrong, but that it would be a mistake to interpret everything that the Bible says literally. This brought even more criticism against Galileo because, at that time, only priests were allowed to interpret the Bible. He was then charged with heresy, which is a belief or opinion that is against the accepted belief of the time. This was a serious accusation at the time, and others had been put to death for similar charges of heresy. Galileo was, however, found innocent of all charges, and he was told to never again teach Copernicus's ideas.

Many years later, Galileo used his telescope and other inventions to measure the movements of Jupiter's moons and prove more concretely the movements of objects in the sky. He was then charged with heresy again and, likely because of his fame, he lived the rest of his life under house arrest rather than facing more serious punishment. It was not until 1992 that the Church formally and publicly cleared Galileo of having committed any crime.

Copernican System

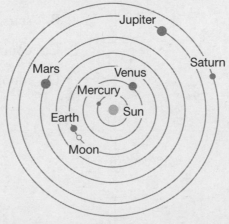

The diagram shows the way Nicolaus Copernicus
theorized the positions of the sun and planets.

1. What is the main idea of the passage?

   A. Nicolaus Copernicus's theory about the universe was correct.

   B. Galileo Galilei invented the telescope.

   C. Galileo Galilei was an influential inventor and astronomer.

   D. In the past, the Church had a lot of influence over the public.

2. Based on the passage, how does the diagram of Copernicus's ideas differ from the more popular model that was accepted by the Church?

   A. The popular model showed Earth as the center of the universe.

   B. The popular model showed Jupiter as the center of the universe.

   C. The popular model showed Earth orbiting the moon.

   D. The popular model showed the sun orbiting all planets.

3. Which statement from the passage is an opinion?

   A. "In addition to viewing Jupiter's rings, Galileo also used his telescope to notice that small objects were revolving around Jupiter."

   B. "His education served him well, because Galileo became one of the greatest thinkers of his time."

   C. "The law of the pendulum was not the only law of science that Galileo explored."

   D. "He was then charged with heresy, which is a belief or opinion that is against the accepted belief of the time."

4. Read the sentence from the passage.

   In addition to viewing Jupiter's rings, Galileo used his telescope to notice that small <u>satellites</u> were revolving around Jupiter.

   What is another word for <u>satellites</u> as used in this sentence?

   A. rings

   B. stars

   C. countries

   D. moons

5. Write a summary of the passage on the lines below.

_____

_____

_____

_____

_____

Read the passage and answer the questions that follow.

excerpted from

The Starry Messenger
by Galileo Galilei

Great indeed are the things which in this brief book that I propose for observation and consideration by all students of nature. I say great, because of the excellence of the subject itself, the entirely unexpected and novel character of the night sky, and finally because of the instrument by means of which they have been revealed to our senses.

Surely it is a great thing to be able to increase the numerous host of stars previously visible to the unaided vision. We hope to add countless more to our vision, which have never before been seen, exposing these plainly to the eye in numbers ten times exceeding the old and familiar stars.

It is a very beautiful thing, and most gratifying to the sight, to behold the body of the moon, distant from us almost sixty earthly radii, as if it were no farther away than two such measures—so that its diameter appears almost thirty times larger, its surface nearly nine hundred times, and its volume twenty-seven thousand times as large as when viewed with the naked eye. In this way one may learn by observation that the moon is not robed in a smooth and polished surface, but is in fact rough and uneven. It is covered everywhere, just like Earth's surface, with huge prominences, deep valleys, and chasms.

Again, it seems to me a matter of no small importance to have ended the dispute about the Milky Way by making its nature obvious to the senses as well as to the intellect. Similarly it will be a pleasant and elegant thing to demonstrate that the nature of those stars which astronomers have previously called "nebulous" is far different from what has been believed until now.

But what surpasses all wonders by far, and what particularly moves us to seek the attention of all astronomers and philosophers, is the discovery of four wandering stars not known or observed by any man before us. Like Venus and Mercury, which have their own periods about the sun, these have theirs about a certain star that is conspicuous among those already known, which they sometimes precede and sometimes follow, without ever departing from it beyond certain limits.

All these facts were discovered and observed by me not many days ago with the aid of a spyglass which I devised, after first being illuminated by divine grace. Perhaps other remarkable things will soon be discovered by me or by other observers with the aid of one of these instruments. I shall first briefly explain this instrument, as well how I developed it. Afterward I shall relate the story of the observations I have made.

About ten months ago a report reached my ears that a certain man from Belgium had constructed a spyglass that allowed visible objects, though very distant from the eye of the observer, to be distinctly seen as if nearby. A few days later the report was confirmed to me in a letter from a noble Frenchman at Paris, Jacques Badovere. The news caused me to apply myself wholeheartedly to inquire into the means by which I might arrive at the invention of a similar instrument.

This I did shortly afterward, my basis being the theory of refraction. First I prepared a tube of lead, at the ends of which I fitted two glass lenses, both plane on one side, while on the other side one was spherically convex and the other concave. Then placing my eye near the concave lens I perceived objects satisfactorily large and near, for they appeared three times closer and nine times larger than when seen with the naked eye alone. Next I constructed another one, more accurate, which represented objects as enlarged more than sixty times. Finally, sparing neither labor nor expense, I succeeded in constructing for myself so excellent an instrument that objects seen by means of it appeared nearly one thousand times larger and over thirty times closer than when regarded with our natural vision.

It would be unnecessary to mention how important such an instrument would be at sea as well as on land. But forsaking terrestrial observations, I turned my spyglass to the sky, and first I saw the moon from as near at hand as if it were scarcely two terrestrial radii away. After that I observed often with wondering delight both the planets and the fixed stars, and since I saw these latter to be very crowded, I began to seek (and eventually found) a method by which I might measure their distances apart.

6. What was the first step in the process that Galileo describes for making his spyglass?

   A. He looked into the night sky.

   B. He prepared a concave lens.

   C. He prepared a tube of lead.

   D. He prepared a convex lens.

7. What is the text structure of the passage?

   A. cause and effect

   B. sequence

   C. compare and contrast

   D. problem and solution

8. Which phrase from the passage helps readers understand the technical process described by Galileo?

   A. spherically convex

   B. similar instrument

   C. divine grace

   D. polished surface

9. Which of the following is NOT a supporting detail in the passage?

   A. Images in the last spyglass appeared to be nearly one thousand times larger than with our natural vision.

   B. Images in the last spyglass appeared to be over thirty times closer than with our natural vision.

   C. There is a way to make stars and other objects in the sky appear closer than they really are.

   D. A man from Belgium constructed a spyglass to make objects appear farther away.

10. What is the reason Galileo used his new spyglass to look at the sky?

   A. The objects in space had never before been seen with a telescope.

   B. The objects in space were much larger than objects on Earth.

   C. No one had ever looked at the night sky before.

   D. There were too many people already looking out at objects at sea.

11. Write a summary of this passage on the lines below.

_____

_____

_____

_____

_____

12. In what ways are the passages "Galileo Galilei: A Scientist's Life" and the excerpt from *The Starry Messenger* alike and different?

_____

_____

_____

_____

_____

_____

_____

_____

8 Main Idea and Supporting Details

RI.6.2, RI.6.10, RH.6.2, RH.6.10, RST.6.2, RST.6.10

Getting the Idea

A **main idea** is the most important idea in a text. It is what a passage is mostly about. A **supporting detail** is a fact that describes, explains, or strengthens the main idea of a text. Read the following paragraph.

> Entering middle school can be both a fun and difficult time in a student's life. Students have the chance to make new friends, join clubs, and gain more independence. There are usually activities, such as dances and school trips. On the downside, not all students adjust quickly to their new situation. They may have trouble making friends. Some will struggle with the greater workload and difficulty of the assignments. Middle school often brings increased social pressures, like choosing the right clothes. For many students, middle school is a balance between the good and the bad.

The main idea of this paragraph is the first sentence.

> Entering middle school can be both a fun and difficult time in a student's life.

The supporting details are the examples that back up this idea. For instance, choosing which clubs to join and participating in school trips support the idea that middle school can be a fun time.

The examples of having trouble making friends, struggling with the school workload, and dealing with the pressures of trying to fit in support the idea that middle school can also be a difficult time.

A **summary** is a short retelling of a text in the reader's own words. A summary includes the main idea and the most important details from the passage that support the main idea. A summary does not include the reader's opinion about the passage. The following summary can be used to describe the paragraph on the previous page.

> There are positive and negative things about entering middle school. The positive things include meeting new friends and taking part in fun activities and clubs. The negative things include adjusting to new situations and having extra work and responsibilities.

Now read the following paragraph and think about what you would include in a summary.

> The United States flag is not just a random design of stars and stripes. It has a symbolic design that represents our nation's past and present. The thirteen stripes on the flag represent the thirteen original colonies. The fifty stars represent the fifty states that are part of our country today.

The main idea is that there is a purpose to the pattern of the U.S. flag. The meanings of the symbols should be included in the summary.

Thinking It Through

Read the following paragraph, and then answer the questions that follow.

Thomas Jefferson was such a lover of reading that he had a collection of thousands of books in his home at Monticello. In fact, when the Library of Congress was burned by the British during the War of 1812, Jefferson was able to sell his collection to Congress as a replacement. The Library of Congress is the largest collection of books in the world. It was Jefferson who helped to organize the books by a number system that categorized them by their subject instead of alphabetically by their titles. Today the Library of Congress remains the most important collection of books in the world.

What is the main idea of the passage? What are the supporting details?

_____

_____

_____

_____

_____

HINT   The main idea is what the passage is mainly about. The supporting details help explain the main idea.

Coached Example

Read the passage and answer the questions.

During the twentieth century, the overall temperature of our climate increased by about one degree Fahrenheit. That may not sound like a lot, but over time this change affects many living things and ecosystems. Many scientists are pointing the finger at humans for this climate change. Since we started burning fossil fuels to run factories, drive cars and planes, and heat our homes, the amount of gases in the air has increased. These gases get trapped in the air and are causing an increase in temperatures. So, a search for alternative energy sources is very important. It may even help save our planet.

1. What is the main idea of the passage?

   A. People burn fossil fuels.

   B. People may be causing climate change on Earth.

   C. Alternative energy sources are needed.

   D. Alternative energy may help save our planet.

   HINT Ask yourself what the passage is mainly about.

2. Which sentence is the BEST summary of the passage?

   A. Average Earth temperatures have risen, but one degree Fahrenheit seems insignificant.

   B. Scientists think human activity is to blame for climate change, and alternative energy sources may prevent further change.

   C. People should live without cars and factories and search for alternative energy sources for economic reasons.

   D. Alternative energy sources may solve the problem of gases getting trapped in the atmosphere.

   HINT A summary tells the main concepts of the passage.

Lesson Practice

Use the Reading Guide to help you understand the passage.

Reading Guide

What is the main idea of the passage?

Summarizing what you read can help you find the main idea.

How do the details help to support the main idea?

Go West: The Story of Manifest Destiny

In the United States during the 1840s, politicians and leaders were encouraging citizens to "go west" and explore and settle the land. They began using the phrase "manifest destiny" to describe this policy. Leaders believed that it was our destiny as a country to not just settle in the East around the thirteen original colonies, but to expand all the way westward throughout the entire continent.

It was not hard to understand why some sort of expansion was needed. The United States was growing. New immigrants were coming to the country in droves. Families sprang up everywhere throughout the eastern states, and farmland was becoming scarce. The population of the country was five million in 1800, and by the middle of the century, it was over twenty-three million.

The West represented freedom and opportunity. Most land was very inexpensive, and some of it was even free. There were no local governments and no rules. The land seemed to never end. This meant money for farmers and opportunities for people to start over. Almost four million Americans moved west between 1820 and 1850. The idea of manifest destiny changed the United States. Today Americans have expanded to every corner of the nation.

Answer the following questions.

1. What is the main idea of the passage?

   A. America expanded westward during the 1800s.

   B. The U.S. population increased during the 1800s.

   C. The West represented freedom.

   D. In the 1800s, land in the West was inexpensive.

2. If you were to write a summary of the passage, which word or phrase would be in the summary?

   A. new immigrants

   B. population

   C. farmer

   D. manifest destiny

3. Which detail BEST supports the idea that manifest destiny was a popular idea?

   A. "Most land was very inexpensive, and some of it was even free."

   B. "The land seemed to never end."

   C. "Almost four million Americans moved west between 1820 and 1850."

   D. "There were no local governments and no rules."

4. Where did MOST of the people exploring the West come from?

   A. states in the East

   B. states in the West

   C. European colonies

   D. the Atlantic Ocean

5. Summarize the passage on the lines below.

   _____

   _____

   _____

   _____

9 Text Structures

RI.6.3, RI.6.5, RI.6.10, RH.6.5, RH.6.10, RST.6.10

Getting the Idea

Text structure is the way an author chooses to present information. There are many ways to present nonfiction information, and authors choose their text structure based on their topic. Common text structures include cause and effect, sequence, compare and contrast, and problem and solution.

A **cause-and-effect** text structure gives the reasons and outcomes for events. A **cause** is a person, thing, or event that makes something happen. An **effect** is the result of a cause. For example, a cause-and-effect text structure would work well for a report about the events that led up to the Revolutionary War. Read the following paragraph and identify the causes and effects.

> The British rule had increased taxes on the colonists several times. As a result of these taxes, the colonists planned the Boston Tea Party to show their anger and their independence. The most serious result of the colonists' anger, however, was the outbreak of the Revolutionary War.

The cause in the paragraph is the increased taxes brought on by the British. The effect is the Boston Tea Party and later the Revolutionary War. Look for words such as *because, as a result, since, so that, due to,* and *therefore* to identify causes and effects. One cause may have several effects, and several causes may have just one effect.

Another structure is **sequence**, which is chronological, or time, order. Chronological order is the most common sequence structure in nonfiction. Biographies, procedural texts, and recounts of specific events use the sequence structure. The following paragraph is an example of a text that uses a sequence structure.

> Betsy Ross was born as Elizabeth Griscom on January 1, 1752. She was taught by the Quakers and after school worked in her father's business. In 1773 she married John Ross, and in 1776 she was asked to perform one of the most important jobs an American could do—sew the first American flag.

Look for dates or words such as *first, next, then,* and *last* to identify sequence.

Another common text structure used in nonfiction is **compare and contrast**. This structure tells how two or more things are alike and different. To **compare** means to tell how things are similar. To **contrast** means to tell how things are different. Words such as *like, unlike, different, opposite, same,* and *similar* clue readers that they are reading a text with a compare-and-contrast structure. Read the following paragraph.

> Butterflies and moths are alike in many ways. Both are insects. Both have three body parts, six legs, wings, and antennae. They are also different from each other. Butterflies have slimmer bodies than moths and are usually more colorful. Butterflies have a round knob at the end of their antennae. Moths have feathery antennae. Butterflies are active during the day. Moths are active at night.

The paragraph compares and contrasts butterflies and moths. As you read, think about what similarities and differences you can find between ideas, people, events, and objects.

Problem and solution is another text structure. In this structure, an obstacle, or a challenge, must be overcome or a problem must be solved. The **problem** is the difficult situation, obstacle, or challenge. The **solution** is the answer to the problem. Read the following paragraph.

> In the 1800s, many people wanted to move west as the eastern United States grew crowded. The problem is that it took months to cross the United States by wagon or horse. To solve this problem, the first continental railroad was built. Now people could move in much less time.

The problem is that moving west by wagon or horse was very slow. The solution was the construction of the continental railroad.

Another way an author thinks about presenting information is how the whole text is put together. A text may be written in paragraphs. Each sentence in a paragraph should be related to the information presented. All the paragraphs then should fit together and relate to the main idea of the text. A very long informational text may be separated into chapters. The chapters should fit together and relate to the main idea of the entire book.

Thinking It Through

Read the following paragraph, and then answer the question that follows.

On March 30, 1867, Secretary of State William H. Seward arranged to buy Alaska from Russia for $7.2 million. However, there were many critics of the deal. Even though the United States had paid roughly two cents per acre for the land, many Americans argued that this price was much too high. Another cause of people's complaints was that Alaska was far removed from the rest of the United States and was viewed as a frozen wilderness. They thought buying Alaska was a folly, or foolish act. As a result, the deal became known as "Seward's Folly." However, history would show that Seward was not a fool. In 1968, oil was discovered in Alaska, leading to the construction of the Alaska Pipeline. Since 1977, more than fifteen billion barrels of oil have flowed through the pipeline. Today, Alaska celebrates Seward's Day on the last Monday of March.

What is the text structure of the passage? Tell how you know.

_____

_____

_____

_____

HINT   Look for clue words that give hints about the structure.

Coached Example

Read the passage and answer the questions.

The rock cycle is a process by which rocks form and change from one type to another. The three main rock types are igneous, sedimentary, and metamorphic. Igneous rocks form when hot magma from Earth's crust cools into crystals. Some of these rocks come to Earth's surface usually as a result of a volcanic eruption. Over time, these rocks

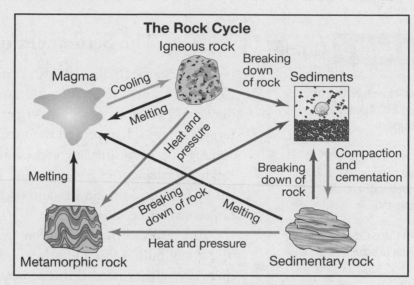

are then broken into pieces, called sediment. The sediment is then buried in layers of earth. Pressure and time cause sedimentary rocks to form. Other igneous rocks remain underground. Pressure and heat from inside Earth change these rocks to metamorphic rocks. Metamorphic rocks can also break down and form sedimentary rocks. Heat, pressure, and time make the rock cycle possible.

---

1. Which text structure is NOT used in the passage?

   A. problem and solution

   B. cause and effect

   C. sequence

   D. compare and contrast

   HINT Review the meaning of each of the structures to see which fits best.

2. Which word from the passage is MOST helpful in identifying a text structure?

   A. process

   B. which

   C. form

   D. rock

   HINT Think about how each word is used in the passage.

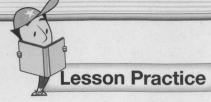

Lesson Practice

Use the Reading Guide to help you understand the passage.

Reading Guide

Look for clues that give you a hint about the text structure.

Is the text telling about one thing, or is it telling how things are alike and different?

Are there dates? Are they given in order?

The Settlement of Jamestown

In the early 1600s, a British company called the Virginia Company wanted to expand and explore new land in hopes that they could make money in other parts of the world. The king of England, James I, approved their trip to the New World in 1606, and a group of businessmen set off to form the first permanent English settlement in America. The 104 settlers arrived in 1607, led by Captain John Smith, and they named their settlement Jamestown after King James.

As a result of the new settlement, many things happened. The group built a fort and other buildings designed to protect themselves. They needed this protection, because the settlers had to deal with attacks from the Algonquin tribe almost as soon as they arrived. The Pawhatan tribe, however, traded with the English settlers and helped them adjust to the new land.

Life was difficult for the new settlers, but the winter of 1609 was particularly harsh. Because of this harsh winter, less than one-fifth of the then five hundred colonists survived. Sixty colonists stayed in the settlement, while thirty-seven others escaped by ship.

But the settlement continued. The people grew crops and sold them to England as well as to Native Americans in the area.

As soon as word got back to England that the Jamestown settlement was beginning to thrive and make money, more settlers came to other parts of the eastern coastline.

Answer the following questions.

1. What kind of text structure is MOSTLY used in the passage?

   A. compare and contrast

   B. cause and effect

   C. sequence

   D. problem and solution

2. What was the overall outcome of the Jamestown settlement?

   A. More crops were grown.

   B. More settlers came to America.

   C. James I became king of England.

   D. Many forts were built in Virginia.

3. Why were there only sixty settlers left after the winter of 1609?

   A. because of the harsh weather

   B. because the Virginia Company wanted to explore

   C. because they were attacked by the Algonquins

   D. because they only grew one crop

4. Which phrase is the BEST clue about the text structure?

   A. in the early 1600s

   B. as a result

   C. but the settlement

   D. as soon as

5. How do the text structures help the author give information?

   _____

   _____

   _____

   _____

   _____

10 Steps in a Process

RI.6.10, RH.6.3, RH.6.10, RST.6.3, RST.6.10

Getting the Idea

In social studies or science texts, an author must sometimes explain to the reader how something is done. This is called **steps in a process**. The author might explain the steps to describe how a bill becomes a law. It might be a step-by-step instruction about how a Native American group made their homes or how they made goods, such as clothing and baskets. Look for key words such as *first, next, then,* and *finally* that indicate steps in a process. Read the following paragraph.

> There are several steps that a letter handled by the United States Postal Service must go through before it reaches its destination. First, a person leaves the letter in a mail drop-off point, such as a public mailbox or at a local post office. Next, a mail carrier empties the box and delivers all of the contents to a central location where the letters are sorted by their zip codes and ultimate destination. Then, the letters are transferred to the post offices closest to their destinations. The letters are then sorted again according to their addresses. Finally, a mail carrier delivers the letter to the addressee.

In texts that explain the steps in a process, the author's opinion is not given, and the history of the topic is not explored. The text simply states the process step-by-step.

In science texts, the author must sometimes explain how a process of nature works or how to do an experiment.

Multistep instructions tell a reader how to make or do something. Many multistep instructions are numbered and include only the text needed for the instruction.

On the next page is a simple process that shows how to make your own temporary compass. A compass is a tool for showing directions, such as north, south, east, and west.

To make your own temporary compass, follow this set of instructions:

1. Carefully rub a three-inch sewing needle against a bar magnet a few times, always in the same direction.

2. Pierce the needle through the center of a cork, from the top to the bottom of the cork.

3. Place the cork and needle on its side in a bowl of water so that it floats.

4. Do not touch the cork again. It will move at first and then finally stop when the needle faces magnetic north.

5. The charge of the magnet moves to the needle, and the needle becomes magnetized temporarily.

Notice that the steps are written in order. This allows the reader to follow the steps one at a time, from beginning to end. Sometimes explanations can be given before or after the instructions to explain the process or to tell why it must be done in a certain way.

Thinking It Through

Read the following passage, and then answer the question that follows.

How to Show Why the Sky Is Blue

1. Gather the following materials: a clear glass or plastic bottle with straight sides, water, milk, measuring spoons, and a flashlight.

2. Add water until the container is three-quarters full.

3. Add one teaspoon of milk. Shake or stir the container until the milk dissolves to form a solution.

4. Turn on the flashlight and turn off the lights in the room. Hold the flashlight above the container as if it is the sun shining directly down through the atmosphere.

5. Notice that the liquid looks blue. The milk is like dust in our atmosphere. It scatters the light, which is made up of red, orange, yellow, green, blue, indigo, and violet waves. Only the blue light can be seen in this experiment in the same way that only blue light can be seen in our atmosphere.

Why does the explanation of the activity come at the end of the activity?

_____

_____

_____

_____

HINT   How does the title help you understand the process?

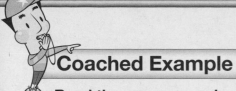

Coached Example

Read the passage and answer the questions.

When a frog lays eggs in water, the animals that are hatched from the eggs do not look anything like frogs. A baby frog is called a tadpole. It has a long tail and lives only in the water, breathing with gills. After about five weeks of growing, the tadpole develops hind legs, and then eventually front legs. As the tadpole grows, its tail gets shorter and the animal begins to grow lungs inside its body. Then, the full-grown frog lives the rest of its life on land and in the water. It has legs, lungs, and no tail. This life cycle starts again when an adult female frog lays eggs.

Frog Life Cycle

1. egg mass   2. tadpole

4. adult frog   3. froglet

---

1. According to the passage and diagram, which step starts the life cycle of a frog?

   A. A tadpole grows hind legs.

   B. An adult frog lays eggs in the water.

   C. A tadpole's tail gets shorter.

   D. A tadpole grows lungs inside its body.

   HINT Reread the beginning of the passage and look at the picture.

2. Which stage comes right before the adult frog is able to live on land?

   A. The tadpole grows hind legs.

   B. The tadpole hatches from an egg.

   C. The tadpole grows lungs, and its tail gets shorter.

   D. The tadpole grows front legs.

   HINT Find the place in the passage that tells about living on land. Then read what happens just before that.

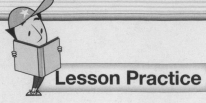

Lesson Practice

Use the Reading Guide to help you understand the passage.

Reading Guide

What information is given in paragraph 1?

Look for clue words that tell you that you are reading about the steps in a process.

Are the steps easy to follow?

Nomination of a Supreme Court Justice

The United States Supreme Court is the highest court in the nation. It is the head of the judicial branch of government. It consists of one chief justice and eight associate justices. The president of the United States is the person who starts the process of choosing who might become a new Supreme Court justice.

The first step in the process of nominating a Supreme Court justice is for one of the nine positions to become open. A Supreme Court justice is appointed for life, so only the death of the justice or his or her retirement would create an opening on the court.

When a position is open, the president chooses a person who he feels would be a good candidate for the job. It is solely up to the president to make this decision. This power is given to the president by Article Two of the U.S. Constitution.

Once a person is chosen, a part of the U.S. Senate called the Senate Judiciary Committee holds hearings, or public interviews, with the nominee to decide if the nomination should be approved. The committee then votes for or against the nomination and gives a report to the entire Senate about the nominee.

Finally, the full Senate conducts a vote to accept or reject the new Supreme Court justice nominee. A simple majority of votes is all that is required.

Answer the following questions.

1. What is the first step in nominating a Supreme Court justice?

   A. The full Senate conducts a vote.

   B. A position becomes available.

   C. The Senate Judiciary Committee holds hearings.

   D. The president chooses a qualified person.

2. When is the president involved in the process?

   A. at the beginning

   B. at the end

   C. through the whole process

   D. never involved

3. Which step comes last in the process of nominating a Supreme Court justice?

   A. The Senate Judiciary Committee holds hearings.

   B. The full Senate conducts a vote.

   C. The Senate Judiciary Committee votes.

   D. The Senate Judiciary Committee submits its views to the Senate.

4. Which branch of government does the Supreme Court lead?

   A. federal

   B. executive

   C. legislative

   D. judicial

5. How does the Senate Judiciary Committee help with the process of appointing a new Supreme Court justice?

   _____

   _____

   _____

   _____

   _____

11 Scientific and Technical Texts

RI.6.4, RI.6.10, RH.6.4, RH.6.10, RST.6.1, RST.6.2, RST.6.4, RST.6.5, RST.6.6, RST.6.10

Getting the Idea

Scientific and technical texts are texts that include science lessons, scientific experiments, and instruction manuals. For example, when you read a manual that tells you how to set up or use your cell phone, you are reading a technical text. This kind of text uses very specific vocabulary that you may not see when you read anything else. Some manuals use symbols to indicate when an action must be taken on your part to set something up. Other symbols indicate when you are about to do something that could be dangerous. Numbered diagrams may help to familiarize the reader with the parts of a technical device such as a computer, video camera, or an ice cream maker. Capital letters sometimes call out certain features or buttons.

Read the following technical text.

1. To start the phone, hold the POWER button down until the screen lights up and the company icon appears.

2. Press the MENU button to make the main menu appear.

3. Choose one of the following features: PHONE, E-MAIL, VIDEO, WEB, or TEXT.

4. Follow this guide to find the instructions for each of the above menu options.

PHONE	E-MAIL	VIDEO	WEB	TEXT
p. 2	p. 3	p. 4	p. 5	p. 7

This technical text uses numbered steps to give instructions, and it uses capital letters to indicate the names of the buttons on the phone. The table then refers the reader to places in the manual where more detailed instructions can be found.

Word choice is when an author's choice of words is used to create a particular meaning. Good word choice is not about using fancy or complicated words. It is about choosing the right words for what you are trying to say. Scientific and technical texts require that word choices fit the topic being discussed.

The following chart lists some words you may find in specific subject areas.

Subject Area-Specific Words

Technical	Science	Social Studies
download	hypothesis	electorate
activate	prediction	primary election
domain	data	culture
calibrate	analysis	political

Read the following text.

> When a scientist works in the field, he or she must write accurate records of observations. It is these written observations that will become the basis for analysis as well as scrutiny by colleagues. For example, if a scientific observation of gorillas in their natural habitat does not include the date, time, and physical description of the habitat, including temperature and weather conditions, the data is much less useful than if it has these important markers.

In this paragraph, the author chose words that would be most useful for the reader to understand the main idea of the text. Words such as *observations, analysis, scrutiny,* and *colleagues* can help the reader understand the technical nature of the text. Words such as *habitat* and *data* also help the reader understand the scientific text. These words are the accurate, precise words for the subject area.

Thinking It Through

Read the following paragraph, and then answer the question that follows.

Chopsticks are tools used for eating in many Asian cultures, in the same way that Americans use a fork or a spoon. The correct way to use chopsticks is to hold them toward the wider end. There are basic rules for using chopsticks. You should never pierce food with a chopstick. This is considered very offensive. You should also never point your chopstick at someone or move food with chopsticks. This is considered very rude. If you need to move food from your bowl to another person's bowl, turn your chopsticks around. This way you are not touching the food with the part of the chopstick that has been in contact with your mouth.

Why is this paragraph considered a technical text?

_____

_____

_____

_____

HINT   Review the definition of technical texts and when they are used.

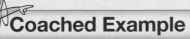

Coached Example

Read the passage and answer the questions.

Read the ballot directions carefully. If you need help with the voting machine, ask an election official for help. Once entering the voting booth, review each candidate's name in the top left corner of the ballot. To cast your vote, press the button with the √ next to your choice. Each candidate's name is listed to the right of one of the buttons. You may cast only one vote, and vote for only one candidate. Another vote will not register if you press a second button. If you make a mistake, ask an election official to reset the screen for you so you may begin again.

1. Which word in the passage must be understood in order to cast a vote?

   A. candidate

   B. register

   C. reset

   D. official

   HINT Think about what the directions are about and what the reader is trying to do.

2. How does the √ in the paragraph help the reader understand the directions?

   A. It helps the reader know how to write on the ballot.

   B. It helps the reader explain the ballot to others.

   C. It helps the reader recognize symbols on the ballot.

   D. It helps the reader know how to fix mistakes.

   HINT Reread the text to understand how the symbols are used.

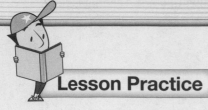

Lesson Practice

Use the Reading Guide to help you understand the passage.

Reading Guide

How do the numbered steps give you a hint about the kind of writing?

Think about the author's purpose for writing the steps in order.

Are there any subject area-specific words?

How to Grow Rock Crystals

Follow these steps to grow your own crystals. For step 2, get the help of an adult when boiling water.

1. Cut several sponges into various shapes about two-inches long. Place the sponge pieces in a pie dish, leaving a small amount of space between each piece.

2. Bring a pot of water to a boil. Mix one-quarter cup Epsom salt to each half-cup of water in the pot.

3. Add a single drop of food coloring to the mixture.

4. Pour the hot mixture of colored, salted water slowly and evenly over the pieces of sponge in the pie dish.

5. Place the pie dish in a windowsill or other location that gets sunlight.

6. Observe the sponge pieces each day and record your results.

7. The rock crystals should form as water evaporates from the mixture. The crystals will take a few days to form, but your observations should span a full week.

8. Make a chart to record your observations. Each day, measure any crystals you see and record the data on your chart.

Answer the following questions.

1. Which step comes before boiling a pot of water?

    A. measuring crystals

    B. adding food coloring to the water

    C. cutting sponges

    D. recording observations

2. Which step BEST explains what will happen during the activity?

    A. 1

    B. 5

    C. 7

    D. 8

3. Which word is a science word that helps explain why the crystals form?

    A. measure

    B. evaporates

    C. form

    D. record

4. Which steps of the experiment involve measuring?

    A. 2

    B. 4

    C. 3 and 6

    D. 2 and 8

5. Do you think the experiment would work without step 5? Why or why not?

    _____

    _____

    _____

    _____

    _____

12 Graphics

RI.6.10, RH.6.7, RH.6.10, RST.6.7, RST.6.10

Getting the Idea

A **graphic** is an image that helps you better understand the written information in a text. Some graphics will have captions. A **caption** is a small amount of text that explains what is shown in the graphic. In a social studies text, some graphics you will find are pictures, maps, and timelines.

A **picture** gives a visual representation of what something looks like. A picture can be a photograph or an illustration that shows you important people, places, events, or things from history.

In social studies, you also learn where places, such as cities and countries, are located. A **map** is a drawing of a location. The map below shows the location of streets in Lancaster, Pennsylvania. You can see that the former home of President James Buchanan is marked on the map at 1120 Marietta Avenue.

WHEATLAND, the former home of President James Buchanan

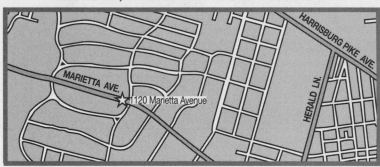

A **timeline** is a list of events organized by date. A timeline can be a bulleted list that is read from top to bottom, or a line with marked dates read from left to right.

Important Dates in Astronomy

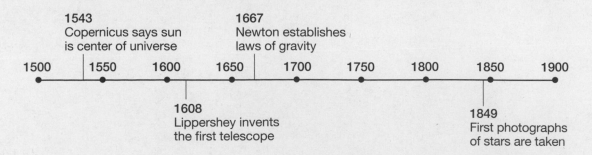

You will also see graphics in a science text. Some common graphics are flowcharts, diagrams, and tables.

A **flowchart** shows the sequence of events. A science text may use a flowchart to show the steps in a process, such as the flow of energy.

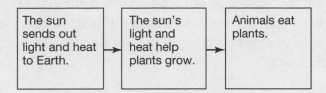

A **diagram** is a drawing with labels. A diagram can help clarify written information in the text. It can also provide extra information that is not discussed directly in the text. A diagram helps show the parts of something.

Animal Cell

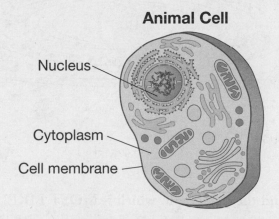

A **table** is a chart that shows information in columns and rows. Tables can quickly summarize information. A common table found in science texts is the Mohs' scale of mineral hardness.

Mineral	Hardness
talc	1
gypsum	2
calcite	3
fluorite	4
apatite	5
feldspar	6
quartz	7
topaz	8
corundum	9
diamond	10

Thinking It Through

Read the following paragraph, and then answer the question that follows.

The most distinctive feature of our solar system is the eight planets that orbit the sun. Each planet's distance from the sun contributes to that planet's physical features. For example, the planets close to the sun have higher temperatures than those that are farther away.

Our Solar System

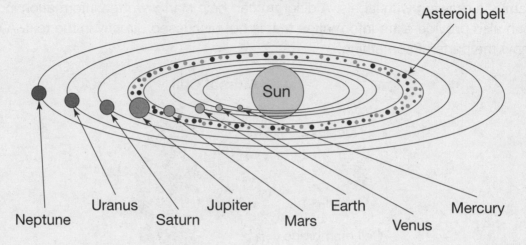

According to the diagram and the paragraph, which is MOST LIKELY to be the coldest planet? Explain your answer.

_____

_____

_____

_____

HINT   Read the passage and view the planet names to find the answer to the question.

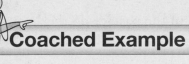

Coached Example

Read the passage and the diagram, and answer the questions.

The Water Cycle

The water cycle is a continuous cycle that describes the movement of water on and above Earth's surface. Because it is a continuous cycle, there is no true starting point. However, first think about the water in the ocean. As the sun heats this water, the water evaporates into the air and becomes a gas. It becomes part of the atmosphere. Then as the air cools, the gas condenses into tiny droplets, and clouds are formed. When these clouds get too heavy with water, they fall to the ground as precipitation. Rain, snow, hail, and sleet are all kinds of precipitation. When precipitation falls onto mountains and hills, it runs downhill and eventually makes its way into the ocean again.

You see the water cycle at work when you see a puddle after a rainstorm. The puddle will soon disappear because the sun's heat will cause the water to evaporate into the air. As the water cycle continues, that once-liquid puddle will soon condense into a cloud and eventually fall again as precipitation.

This evaporation, condensation, and precipitation cycle makes up the water cycle.

Water Cycle Diagram

The Water Cycle

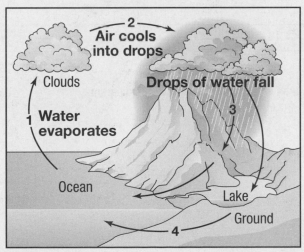

1. How are the passage and the diagram related?

   A. They give different information.

   B. They give the same information in different ways.

   C. The give different information in the same way.

   D. They are not related.

   HINT Use both the diagram and the text to help you find the correct answer.

2. What idea in the passage do the arrows in the diagram help to illustrate?

   A. There are many stages to the water cycle.

   B. The water cycle can be stopped at any stage.

   C. There is no beginning or end to the cycle.

   D. The clouds are an important part of the water cycle.

   HINT Think about the movement shown by the arrows, and reread the text to find the correct answer.

3. How does the diagram help to make the text clearer?

   _____

   _____

   _____

   _____

   _____

   HINT Summarize what you have learned by looking at the diagram.

Lesson Practice

Use the Reading Guide to help you understand the passage.

Reading Guide

Look for dates that might be used in a graphic, such as a table, timeline, or flowchart.

The text should help to clarify and give more details about what you see in the graphic on the next page.

Which graphics would help you organize the information in the passage?

Actions that Led to World War I

We may look back at the events of World War I and wonder how such a huge dispute between nations ever erupted in the first place. The events that led up to the war date back to an important event in Sarajevo (the present-day capital of Bosnia-Herzegovina) on June 28, 1914. The heir to the throne of Austria-Hungary, Archduke Franz Ferdinand, was assassinated as he arrived at the Sarajevo Town Hall.

A Serbian secret society called the Black Hand was responsible for the assassination. The Serbian government denied that this group was part of their government. However, in an effort to seek justice for the crime that was committed against their nation, the Austro-Hungarian government presented an ultimatum to the Serbian government. If the assassins were not brought to justice, the nation would lose its right to govern itself.

The refusal to meet the ultimatum caused both parties to seek approval and assurance from their allies in case a war should erupt between the two nations. The Serbians were closely tied to the Russians, and the Austro-Hungarian government had close ties to Germany.

On July 28, 1914, Austria-Hungary declared war on Serbia. Russia and Germany soon mobilized their armies. Many other nations, such as France, Great Britain, and the United States, would later get involved in the war.

World War I Timeline

The following timeline shows some events that led up to World War I, and how the United States eventually became involved.

Compare the dates and events on the timeline to the dates and events in the passage.

Which events on the timeline are not mentioned in the passage?

Is the timeline easier to understand than the passage?

June 28, 1914: Heir to the Austro-Hungarian throne Archduke Franz Ferdinand is assassinated in Sarajevo.

July 5, 1914: German Kaiser Wilhelm II promises support to Austria in its conflict against Serbia.

July 28, 1914: Austria-Hungary declares war on Serbia.

August 1, 1914: Germany declares war on Russia because of Russia's alliance with Serbia.

August 3, 1914: Germany declares war on France and invades Belgium because of Belgium's alliance with Russia.

August 4, 1914: Due to the German invasion of Belgium, Great Britain declares war on Germany.

May 7, 1915: German submarine sinks the British ocean liner *Lusitania*. Many Americans on board are killed.

April 6, 1917: U.S. President Woodrow Wilson, with Congress's support, declares war on Germany.

Answer the following questions.

1. Which countries were involved in the very first events that led to World War I?

    A. Germany and France

    B. Serbia and Austria-Hungary

    C. Russia and Germany

    D. Austria-Hungary and Germany

2. According to the timeline, which event occurred in July 1914?

    A. German Kaiser Wilhelm II promises support to Austria in its conflict against Serbia.

    B. Great Britain declares war on Germany.

    C. Germany declares war on Russia because of Russia's alliance with Serbia.

    D. Germany declares war on France.

3. Why did Russia and Germany get involved in the disagreement?

    A. They knew who killed Archduke Ferdinand.

    B. Serbia forced them both into helping.

    C. They both had ties to the countries involved.

    D. Austria-Hungary asked them both to help.

4. What information does the timeline give that the passage does not?

    A. Details about Austria-Hungary's ultimatum to Serbia.

    B. The date that Archduke Ferdinand was killed.

    C. The date that war was declared on Serbia.

    D. How and when the United States became involved in the war.

5. How does the timeline help to support the information in the passage?

    _____

    _____

    _____

    _____

13 Author's Argument

RI.6.8, RI.6.10, RH.6.6, RH.6.8, RH.6.10, RST.6.8, RST.6.10

Getting the Idea

Sometimes an author will write to persuade an audience of his or her opinion. An author's **argument** is the way an author presents an opinion in writing. Author's arguments use **persuasion**, which is a way to change how a reader thinks, acts, or feels about something.

In science and social studies texts, an author may make claims that help to support an argument. The author must support these claims with reasons and evidence. With a text that uses persuasion, it is important to distinguish what is a fact and what is an opinion.

A **fact** is a statement that can be proved to be true or false.

There are fifty states in the United States of America.

An **opinion** is a statement that cannot be proved. Not everyone will agree with others' opinions.

Hawaii is the best state to live in.

When an author gives an opinion, he or she may show **bias**, which means that the writer is prejudiced toward one point of view and tries to sway the reader to accept it. **Propaganda techniques** are ways that a writer can use bias to convince the reader of a certain point of view. The following chart shows different propaganda techniques.

Propaganda Technique	Definition	Example
bandwagon	convincing a reader to do something because everyone else is doing it	Don't be the only one who doesn't support our cause!
inclusion or avoidance of particular facts	mentioning only facts that will help to persuade people to your opinion	Forty percent of the students complained about the program within the first three days.
loaded language	language that appeals to emotions rather than reason	This will be a life-changing event.

Facts and opinions are often used in advertising to convince a person to buy or do something. But these techniques can also be found within historical and scientific texts. Read the following paragraph and see if you can distinguish fact from opinion.

> Think about the great health benefits of fruit. Fruit is made of 80 percent water, and water is needed for healthy bodies. Fruit has no "bad cholesterol," which is also very good news for our bodies. Many people say that fruit is good brain food, and that it helps people think more clearly. Fruit also contains fiber. Fiber is good for digestion. Fruit always makes people feel better, too.

In the paragraph, facts about fruit are presented in a persuasive way, and no negative information or facts are included. The last sentence is an opinion because it states what the author believes. However, some people have fruit allergies, and eating fruit would actually make them feel worse.

Read the next paragraph and identify the author's argument.

> In 1967, a man named Steve Juneau came up with an idea to promote the city of Gonzales, Louisiana. He loved how area cooks prepared jambalaya. Jambalaya is a tasty Cajun-Creole dish with a delicious blend of meats and flavors. Why not use this dish to draw people to Gonzales? That's how the annual Jambalaya Festival came to be. In 1968, the governor of Louisiana named Gonzales the "Jambalaya Capital of the World." That same year, the first festival was held. Thirteen cooks competed for the title of "World Jambalaya Cooking Champion." About 15,000 people attended the festival. There were pots of jambalaya, a carnival for the children, and live music. Everyone had a wonderful time. Over time, the festival grew in popularity and reputation. One recent festival drew over 50,000 people.

The paragraph uses mainly facts, such as dates and people's names, to present the information. The paragraph also uses emotional, loaded language, such as *delicious* and *wonderful*, to persuade the reader to believe that the festival was a wonderful idea and a great success.

Thinking It Through

Read the following paragraph, and then answer the questions that follow.

Littering rivers causes the water to become polluted. Pollution harms the fish, plants, and animals that live in or near the river. The plants and animals can get sick and even become extinct. We all need to remember that we are not alone on this planet. We are not the most important species on Earth. What we do affects other living things. If an animal depends on a particular plant for its food, and that plant is no longer around, that animal will have to find another food source or die. We must always be mindful of how our actions affect other living things on the planet.

What is the author's argument? How do the facts in the paragraph support the author's argument?

_____

_____

_____

_____

HINT Determine which statements in the paragraph are facts. How do the facts support the author's main argument?

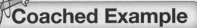

Coached Example

Read the passage and answer the questions.

East Town Shores is the ideal place to visit and to live. It offers the best of everything, from tree-lined streets and peaceful parks to museums, movie theaters, and fine restaurants. East Town Shores has something for everyone. It is home to people of all different walks of life. What's most important is that the town reflects the history of our nation's earliest days. If you are a history buff who wants to learn more about how this nation started, a visit to East Town Shores is just what you need.

1. Which sentence from the passage is a fact?

   A. "East Town Shores is the ideal place to visit and to live."

   B. "It offers the best of everything, from tree-lined streets and peaceful parks to museums, movie theaters, and fine restaurants."

   C. "It is home to people of all different walks of life."

   D. "If you are a history buff who wants to learn more about how this nation started, a visit to East Town Shores is just what you need."

   HINT Find a sentence that avoids the author's personal feelings or beliefs.

2. What is the author trying to convince the reader to do?

   A. visit a fine restaurant

   B. walk in a peaceful park

   C. learn more about history

   D. visit East Town Shores

   HINT What is the author's main purpose?

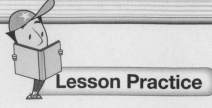

Lesson Practice

Use the Reading Guide to help you understand the passage.

Reading Guide

What does the phrase "dirty politicians" tell you about the author's argument and opinions?

What propaganda techniques does the author use?

Which words or phrases help you identify the author's argument?

The Teapot Dome Scandal

If you have ever wondered where the phrase "dirty politicians" comes from, you might look back to the Teapot Dome Scandal of the 1920s.

The controversy arose in 1921 over control of oil reserves called Teapot Dome, located on public land in Wyoming. The controls were transferred from the United States Navy to the Department of the Interior in 1921. That in itself is not enough to cause a problem, but by 1922, Secretary of the Interior Albert B. Fall leased the fields to a private oil company. This was done without bids from other competitive companies.

As it turned out, Fall was given very large, interest-free, personal loans from the oil company. Fall's change in lifestyle made it clear that he was given large sums of money. The Senate began to investigate Fall and his actions. Where did this money come from? Why were the oil fields handed over to a private operator so quietly and easily?

The Teapot Dome Scandal was one of the first times in U.S. history that politicians were charged with questionable behavior and for making political decisions in exchange for personal favors.

Today we expect to view politicians with a degree of suspicion. We have seen political scandals far too often. But this scandal was one of the first of its kind. Albert B. Fall may well have caused the first "fall" of the honest politician.

Answer the following questions.

1. The author does not mention anything positive Albert B. Fall accomplished in his career in order to show that he was dishonest. What kind of propaganda technique is this?

   A. bandwagon

   B. inclusion of facts

   C. avoidance of facts

   D. loaded language

2. What evidence from the text shows that Albert B. Fall's actions were considered a scandal?

   A. The Senate investigated his actions.

   B. Oil reserves are located in Wyoming.

   C. The U.S. Navy had control over the oil fields before 1921.

   D. Albert B. Fall was the Secretary of the Interior.

3. Which statement from the passage cannot be proved?

   A. "Today we expect to view politicians with a degree of suspicion."

   B. "But this scandal was one of the first of its kind."

   C. "Albert B. Fall leased the fields to a private oil company."

   D. "As it turned out, Fall was given very large, interest-free, personal loans from the oil company."

4. Read the following sentence from the passage.

   Albert B. Fall may well have caused the first "fall" of the honest politician.

   What kind of propaganda technique is the statement?

   A. bias

   B. bandwagon

   C. avoidance of facts

   D. loaded language

5. What argument is the author trying to make in the passage?

   _____

   _____

   _____

   _____

   _____

14 Comparing and Contrasting Informational Texts

RI.6.6, RI.6.7, RI.6.9, RI.6.10, RH.6.1, RH.6.2, RH.6.9, RH.6.10, RST.6.9, RST.6.10, W.6.9, WHST.6.9

Getting the Idea

An **author's purpose** is the reason an author writes. One reason an author might write is to inform the reader about a topic. There are two types of informational sources—primary and secondary.

Primary Sources

A **primary source** is a first-hand account of a topic of interest or event. Historical documents that are created by the people who lived through an event are primary sources. Common primary sources include journals, diaries, interviews, letters, speeches, news film footage, autobiographies, memoirs, poetry, drama, music, and art. A primary source is usually written in the first-person point of view. The **first-person point of view** uses the pronoun *I*.

One example of a primary source is *The Diary of Anne Frank*. This is a first-hand account of a girl living through World War II.

Secondary Sources

A **secondary source** is a document that gives information about a person or event in history but is written after the events have occurred. Authors often use primary sources to put together a secondary source. Secondary sources often interpret or analyze primary sources. Common secondary sources include magazine articles, encyclopedias, textbooks, book reports, biographies, and books about nonfiction topics. A secondary source is written in the **third-person point of view**. The third-person point of view uses the pronouns *he, she,* or *they*.

One example of a secondary source is a magazine article that a reporter writes about the life of Anne Frank.

You can compare and contrast information from different sources to tell how they are alike and different. Remember that to **compare** means to tell how things are alike. To **contrast** means to tell how things are different.

Read the following primary source letter written by Abraham Lincoln.

Mrs. Bixby, Boston, Massachusetts:

DEAR MADAM: I have been shown in the files of the War Department a statement of the Adjutant-General of Massachusetts that you are the mother of five sons who have died gloriously on the field of battle. I feel how weak and fruitless must be any words of mine which should attempt to beguile you from the grief of a loss so overwhelming. But I cannot refrain from tendering to you the consolation that may be found in the thanks of the Republic they died to save. I pray that our Heavenly Father may assuage the anguish of your bereavement, and leave you only the cherished memory of the loved and lost, and the solemn pride that must be yours to have laid so costly a sacrifice upon the altar of freedom.

Yours very sincerely and respectfully,
Abraham Lincoln

Now read the following secondary source about the same topic.

Abraham Lincoln led the country at one of its most difficult times. The American Civil War was a time of great heartache for many families. They lost their loved ones on the battlefield, and both sides were fighting for the same country. Lincoln felt overwhelmed by the pride and dignity that many of the soldiers exhibited. He would write personal letters to family members to thank them for the service their loved ones gave to the country.

Both passages are about Abraham Lincoln's dedication to the soldiers of the Civil War. The first passage shows first hand how Lincoln felt, and the second passage gives a second-hand account of the same information.

Thinking It Through

Read the following passage, and then answer the questions that follow.

You may not know the name Josh Gibson, but he was the greatest hitter in the history of baseball. He is often called the black Babe Ruth because he was able to hit long home runs. Some feel that Ruth instead should be called the white Josh Gibson. It was not unusual for Gibson to hit the ball more than five hundred feet. Gibson's records are not remembered in major league baseball because he played for the Negro Leagues.

Gibson was born in Buena Vista, Georgia, in 1911. His first love was always baseball. He started his career when he was asked to step into a Negro Leagues game after a catcher hurt his finger during the game. By the end of his career, some people say that Gibson hit as many as eighty-four home runs in one season. No one knows for certain because the Negro League could not afford to hire someone to keep the records.

What kind of source is this passage? How can you tell?

_____

_____

_____

_____

HINT   Review the meaning of a primary and secondary source and think about the characteristics of each.

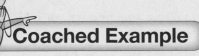

Coached Example

Read the passages and answer the questions.

The Life of Laura Ingalls Wilder

Laura Ingalls Wilder was born in a log cabin in the Wisconsin woods during the winter of 1867. She was the second child of Charles and Caroline Ingalls. She spent much of her childhood traveling across the American frontier with her family. They lived in a dugout house in Walnut Grove, Minnesota, then moved to Iowa where Charles ran a hotel. They later moved back to Walnut Grove, and then finally into the Dakota Territory where her parents settled for the rest of their lives.

Laura wrote about her life story in a series of children's books called *Little House on the Prairie*. The books were written when Laura was an adult, but they have all the memories of childhood and capture the adventures and the dangers of living on the American frontier. Millions of children have read her books since the 1930s.

"Favors of the Small Farm"
excerpted from
Missouri Ruralist (February 18, 1911)
by Mrs. A. J. Wilder

There is a movement in the United States today, widespread, and very far reaching in its consequences. People are seeking after a freer, healthier, happier life. They are tired of the noise and dirt, bad air and crowds of the cities and are turning longing eyes toward the green slopes, wooded hills, pure running water, and health-giving breezes of the country.

A great many of these people are discouraged by the amount of money required to buy a farm and hesitate at the thought of undertaking a new business. But there is no need to buy a large farm. A small farm will bring in a good living with less work and worry, and the business is not hard to learn.

I am an advocate of the small farm, and I want to tell you how an ideal home can be made on, and a good living made from, five acres of land.

1. Which passage is a primary source?

   A. the first passage

   B. the second passage

   C. both passages

   D. neither passage

   HINT Look for the first-person point of view.

2. Which passage is a secondary source?

   A. the first passage

   B. the second passage

   C. both passages

   D. neither passage

   HINT Look for the third-person point of view.

3. How are both passages alike? How are they different?

   _____

   _____

   _____

   _____

   _____

   HINT Compare and contrast the topics and main ideas.

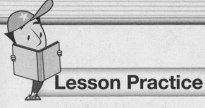

Lesson Practice

Use the Reading Guides to help you understand the passage.

Reading Guide

Think about the point of view of the author.

What is the author's purpose for writing the passage?

What is this passage about?

The Mechanics of Sound

You may not think about it very often, but the sounds you hear all around you are the results of mechanics. That means that sound is a physical process that is a result of forces and motion.

Sound is a mechanical wave, caused by vibrations, a quick back and forth motion, of particles. Sound moves through the air, through water, and through solid objects as well.

If you look at sound waves in action as they move through the air, you would actually be able to see areas where the particles are compressed and other areas where the particles are spread apart, or rarefaction. These waves relate to the pressure in the air.

A wavelength is the distance between the compressions and rarefactions. Since you cannot see the air moving in this way, as shown in the diagram below, you can do an experiment to see particles move in the same pattern as sound waves.

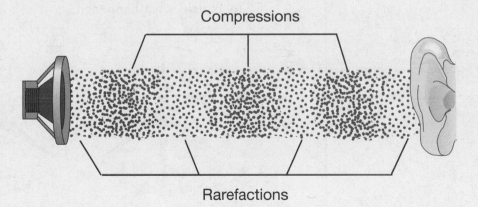

Compressions

Rarefactions

The Shapes of Sounds

What is the author's purpose for writing the passage?

What is this passage about?

Think about how this passage is similar to and different from "The Mechanics of Sound."

You know that sounds travel in waves, but did you know that sounds create geometric shapes and patterns, too? Follow these steps to create your own sound shapes.

1. Pour a cup of sand into an aluminum pie plate.

2. Smooth out the sand so that it is distributed evenly in the plate.

3. Place the plate on top of an electronic amplifier or a speaker if one is available.

4. Plug in the amplifier so that it makes a continuous humming or screeching noise.

5. Record what happens to the sand particles as the frequency and pitch of the sound changes.

6. Draw what you see as the particles of sand react with the vibrations of the sound.

7. Change the sound and again note the changes to the sand particles.

8. Discuss your results with a partner and make a hypothesis to explain what happened.

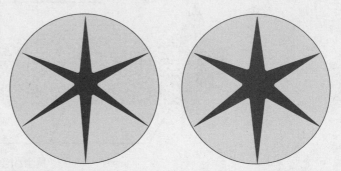

Your sound experiment may create similar geometric shapes out of sand.

Answer the following questions.

1. What do the two passages have in common?

   A. They are both how-to passages.

   B. They are both about sound vibrations.

   C. They are both written in the first person.

   D. They both have the same narrator.

2. Which passage is meant to inform the reader about physical properties of sound?

   A. The Mechanics of Sound

   B. The Shapes of Sounds

   C. neither passage

   D. both passages

3. Which article discusses compression and rarefaction?

   A. The Mechanics of Sound

   B. The Shapes of Sound

   C. neither passage

   D. both passages

4. How does "The Shapes of Sound" provide support for the facts presented in "The Mechanics of Sound"?

   A. It allows the reader to see sound vibrations for himself or herself.

   B. It allows the reader to disprove the concept of rarefaction.

   C. It provides a way to test the strength of sounds.

   D. It provides a way to create sand from sound waves.

5. How did reading "The Mechanics of Sound" help you to better understand the activity in "The Shapes of Sound"?

   _____

   _____

   _____

   _____

   _____

Cumulative Assessment for Lessons 8–14

Read the passage and answer the questions that follow.

excerpted from

Ulysses S. Grant's Personal Memoirs

The 4th of March, 1861, came, and Abraham Lincoln was sworn to maintain the Union against all its enemies. The secession of one state after another followed, until eleven had gone out. On the 11th of April, Fort Sumter, a National fort in the harbor of Charleston, South Carolina, was fired upon by the Southerners and a few days after was captured. The Confederates proclaimed themselves aliens, and thereby debarred themselves of all right to claim protection under the Constitution of the United States. We did not admit the fact that they were aliens, but all the same, they debarred themselves of the right to expect better treatment than people of any other foreign state who make war upon an independent nation. Upon the firing on Sumter, President Lincoln issued his first call for troops and soon after a proclamation convening Congress in extra session. The call was for 75,000 volunteers for ninety days' service. If the shot fired at Fort Sumter "was heard around the world," the call of the president for 75,000 men was heard throughout the Northern States. There was not a state in the North of a million of inhabitants that would not have furnished the entire number faster than arms could have been supplied to them, if it had been necessary.

As soon as the news of the call for volunteers reached Galena, posters were stuck up calling for a meeting of the citizens at the courthouse in the evening. Business ceased entirely; all was excitement; for a time there were no party distinctions; all were Union men, determined to avenge the insult to the national flag. In the evening the courthouse was packed. Although a comparative stranger, I was called upon to preside; the sole reason, possibly, was that I had been in the army and had seen service. With much embarrassment and some prompting, I made out to announce the object of the meeting. Speeches were in order, but it is doubtful whether it would have been safe just then to make other than patriotic ones. There was probably no one in the house, however, who felt like making any other. The two principal speeches were by B. B. Howard, the post-master and a Breckinridge Democrat at the November election the fall before, and John A. Rawlins, an elector on the Douglas ticket. E. B. Washburne, with whom I was not acquainted at that time, came in after the meeting had been organized, and expressed, I understood afterward, a little surprise that Galena could not furnish a presiding officer for such an occasion without taking a stranger. He came forward and was introduced, and made a speech appealing to the patriotism of the meeting.

After the speaking was over, volunteers were called for to form a company. The quota of Illinois had been fixed at six regiments; and it was supposed that one company would be as much as would be accepted from Galena. The company was raised, and the officers and noncommissioned officers elected before the meeting adjourned. I declined the captaincy before the balloting, but announced that I would aid the company in every way I could and would be found in the service in some position if there should be a war. I never went into our leather store after that meeting, to put up a package or do other business.

The ladies of Galena were quite as patriotic as the men. They could not enlist, but they conceived the idea of sending their first company to the field uniformed. They came to me to get a description of the United States uniform for infantry; subscribed and bought the material; procured tailors to cut out the garments, and the ladies made them up. In a few days, the company was in uniform and ready to report at the state capital for assignment. The men all turned out the morning after their enlistment, and I took charge, divided them into squads, and superintended their drill. When they were ready to go to Springfield, I went with them and remained there until they were assigned to a regiment.

There were so many more volunteers than had been called for that the question whom to accept was quite embarrassing to the governor, Richard Yates. The legislature was in session at the time, however, and came to his relief. A law was enacted authorizing the governor to accept the services of ten additional regiments, one from each congressional district, for one month, to be paid by the state, but pledged to go into the service of the United States if there should be a further call during their term. Even with this relief the governor was still very much embarrassed. Before the war was over, he was like the president when he was taken with smallpox: "At last he had something he could give to all who wanted it."

---

1. Which statement from the passage is an opinion?

   A. "Upon the firing on Sumter, President Lincoln issued his first call for troops and soon after a proclamation convening Congress in extra session."

   B. "On the 11th of April, Fort Sumter, a National fort in the harbor of Charleston, South Carolina, was fired upon by the Southerners and a few days after was captured."

   C. "Speeches were in order, but it is doubtful whether it would have been safe just then to make other than patriotic ones."

   D. "After the speaking was over, volunteers were called for to form a company."

2. Read the following statement.

   The ladies of Galena were quite as patriotic as the men.

   How does the author's word choice affect the mood of the paragraph?

   A. It helps the reader to understand that Grant is angry.

   B. It helps the reader to understand that Grant is encouraged.

   C. It helps the reader to understand the meaning of the word *patriotic*.

   D. It helps the reader to understand why Grant is involved in the war.

3. What is the main idea of the passage's last paragraph?

   A. There were not enough volunteers for the regiments.

   B. There were more volunteers for the regiments than could be accepted.

   C. A law was enacted to allow ten additional regiments.

   D. The governor eventually became sick before the end of the war.

4. Which supporting detail shows how much the Union was supported?

   A. The Confederates proclaimed themselves aliens.

   B. Abraham Lincoln was sworn to maintain the Union against all its enemies.

   C. Speeches were in order.

   D. In the evening the courthouse was packed.

5. Write a summary of the passage on the lines below.

   _____

   _____

   _____

   _____

   _____

   _____

Read the passage and answer the questions that follow.

How the Constitution Is Amended

When the United States was in its infancy, the founders of the nation knew that a document would be needed that would state the general laws that should be followed by its citizens. The United States Constitution is a plan for our government. It lays out the structure, the organization, and the basic rights of our people.

Adopted on September 17, 1787, at the Constitutional Convention in Philadelphia, Pennsylvania, the document defines the three main branches of our government: the legislative, the executive, and the judicial branches.

Almost as soon as the Constitution was signed, however, people knew that the rights of citizens were not well defined. Amendments, or changes, to the Constitution were needed. Since the original document was signed, the Constitution has been amended twenty-seven times. The first ten of these changes were passed at the same time and are known as the Bill of Rights.

The Bill of Rights guarantees some of our most important rights as Americans. It guarantees rights such as freedom of speech, freedom of religion, the right to bear arms, and the right to a trial. These are personal rights and protections that are so much part of our way of life that today we often take them for granted. But the founders of the country thought about how our specific rights should be put into law, and the result was the Bill of Rights. When lawsuits are brought against people, the Bill of Rights is sometimes used to defend or protect the citizen being charged. Some of these amendments are rights that had been denied to colonists in their fight against the British, and others are rights that people came to this country in hopes of finding when they started their new lives here.

When the Constitution is changed, a law is changed. The first step in amending the Constitution is to draft a bill, which is a proposed law. It might be to guarantee the right to a fair court trial, such as was proposed in the Sixth Amendment. Then, the bill must pass through both houses of the legislature, or Congress. More than a simple majority vote is needed for this stage of the process. A full two-thirds majority is needed in order for the bill to pass to the next stage.

Next, the bill goes to each of the states for approval. Both houses of each state legislature vote on the bill and again, a two-thirds majority vote is needed for the state to officially approve the bill. Once all of the states have decided whether they want to approve or reject the bill, there is one more requirement to meet. Three-fourths of the states need to ratify, or approve, the bill for it to become an amendment to the Constitution.

The process described above is not a simple one. It takes a lot of discussion and debate about the law and its implications before a vote can even take place. It can take states years to make their decisions. For this reason, Congress will often give states a seven-year time limit to vote on the bill and either reject it or push it through.

The process described is the most popular way to pass an amendment. There are a few other ways, but they have never been used. In one special case, another method was used to repeal the Prohibition laws of the 1920s that prevented the manufacture and sale of alcohol. But all other times, the laws have been passed in the same way each time.

The balance between the federal and state governments is important for amending the constitution. A system of checks and balances exists so that the states do not have too much power, and the federal government does not have too much power, either. This balance can be seen in action during the process of amending the Constitution. There have been thirty-three amendments that have received a two-thirds vote from both houses of the federal legislature. But only twenty-seven of these amendments have been ratified by the states. That means that there were six instances where the states did not agree with the bill being proposed. Just as it was designed by the founders of our country, the Constitution grants the states the power to approve or reject amendments that are proposed by Congress.

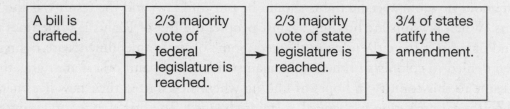

6. Which word from the passage is NOT likely to be found in a science text?

   A. process

   B. ratify

   C. balance

   D. system

7. Which step comes right after a bill is approved by two-thirds of the federal legislature?

   A. It is voted on by the states.

   B. It becomes a law.

   C. It is voted on by three-quarters of states.

   D. It is approved by all of Congress.

8. What kind of graphic is shown in the passage?

   A. table

   B. map

   C. flowchart

   D. timeline

9. What kind of text structure is used in paragraph 5?

   A. cause and effect

   B. sequence

   C. problem and solution

   D. compare and contrast

10. What is the reason that three-fourths of the states have to ratify a bill for it to become an amendment?

   A. so that the federal government does not get too much power

   B. so that the state governments do not get too much power

   C. so that a bill takes a long time to pass

   D. so that all of the amendments are ratified at different times

11. On the lines below, write a summary of the passage.

_____

_____

_____

_____

_____

12. How is the excerpt from Ulysses S. Grant's personal memoirs similar to and different from the passage "How the Constitution Is Amended"?

_____

_____

_____

_____

_____

CHAPTER

3 Writing

Diagnostic Assessment for Lessons 15–19

This passage contains mistakes. Read the passage and answer the questions that follow.

Skyscrapers

(1) New York City is famous for a battle that started in the late 1920s, when two skyscrapers—the Empire State Building and Chrysler Building—were competing for their place in the record books. (2) The Chrysler Building became the tallest building in the world in May of 1930, before the Empire State Building passed it a year later.

(3) All over the world, skyscrapers not only show the flavor of a city, but they are also a symbol of pride for its residents. (4) Ever since cities started building skyscrapers in the 1920s, architects and construction companies have raced to design and build the most striking, tallest skyscraper.

(5) These two buildings were made during a difficult economic time in U.S. history. (6) The Great Depression left many people out of work, so people who were lucky enough to have a job building these magnificent skyscrapers were among the lucky few with jobs. (7) Because of this, many of the workers worked extra hard, knowing that people would be waiting to replace them if they were ever fired. (8) As a result, the Empire State Building was finished well ahead of schedule. (9) It became the pride of the city during a difficult time.

(10) Designing this tower was challenging because Taiwan is often hit by earthquakes and typhoons. (11) Taipei 101 is a skyscraper rising 1,671 feet (or 101 floors) into the sky in Taipei, the capital of Taiwan. (12) To solve this problem architects built a steel sphere weighing eight hundred tons and installed it near the top of the tower. (13) The sphere is supposed to keep the building stable during intense movement, such as what might take place during an earthquake.

(14) Taipei 101 did not hold the record for the highest skyscraper for long. (15) On October 1, 2009, a building in Dubai in the United Arab Emirates became the tallest building in the world. (16) The Burj Dubai, as it was known during construction, took five years to build and had its official grand opening on January 4, 2010. (17) The building has 160 floors that can be occupied as office buildings, and another forty-six maintenance levels located in the tall spire at the top of the building. (18) The project cost $1.5 billion. (19) The distance from the ground to the top of the spire is 2,717 feet, or 828 meters.

(20) It holds more than just a few world records. (21) Not only is world's tallest building, but currently the building is the most floors. (22) It also has the world's highest elevator installation and it is the world's fastest elevator as well. (23) The building also has the world's highest outdoor observation deck, at 1,483 feet, or 452 meters.

(24) The Burj Dubai also has had its share of economic woes, however finished at the height of an economic recession, most of the 160 floors of prime office rental space remains empty.

1. Where would paragraph 1 be better placed in the passage?

   A. after the last paragraph

   B. after paragraph 3

   C. before paragraph 3

   D. before paragraph 5

2. Which paragraph is a good introduction for the passage?

   A. paragraph 1

   B. paragraph 2

   C. paragraph 3

   D. paragraph 4

3. Which question did the student MOST LIKELY ask before starting the research for this passage?

   A. How many windows does a skyscraper have?

   B. Are there skyscrapers in Saudi Arabia?

   C. How many floors does the Willis Tower have?

   D. What are some of the most popular skyscrapers in the world?

4. Which should be the topic sentence of paragraph 4?

   A. sentence 10

   B. sentence 11

   C. sentence 12

   D. sentence 13

5. Paragraph 6 starts with the word *it*. When revising the paragraph, which words should the writer use to replace the word *it*?

   A. the Empire State Building

   B. the Chrysler Building

   C. Taipei 101

   D. Burj Dubai

6. Where can someone look to find current events happening at the Empire State Building?

   A. encyclopedia

   B. atlas

   C. almanac

   D. newspaper

7. Read this sentence from paragraph 6.

   Not only is world's tallest building, but currently the building is the most floors.

   What is the BEST way to rewrite the sentence?

   A. Not only is currently the building with the most floors, it is world's tallest building.

   B. Not only is world's tallest building, but the building has the most current floors.

   C. Not only is it the world's tallest building, but it is currently the building with the most floors.

   D. The world's tallest building, but currently has the most floors.

8. How can paragraph 7 be revised to be clearer for the reader?

   A. Break the paragraph into two or more sentences.

   B. Add more information to the paragraph.

   C. Change the topic of the paragraph.

   D. Make the paragraph part of paragraph 6.

Informative Prompt

Research a person in history whom you respect. Write an essay that explains who the person is and why you respect him or her. Be sure to include specific details.

Use the checklist below to help you do your best writing.

Does your letter

❏ have a clear and focused subject?

❏ have a logical structure?

❏ present information clearly?

❏ use linking words and phrases to join ideas?

❏ use a style and vocabulary that is correct for the audience and purpose?

❏ have a solid conclusion?

❏ have good spelling, capitalization, and punctuation?

❏ follow the rules for good grammar and usage?

Write your response on the next page. Use the space below to organize your information in a graphic organizer.

15 Writing Arguments

W.6.1, W.6.10, WHST.6.1, WHST.6.10

Getting the Idea

Persuasive writing tries to convince the reader of the writer's argument. A writer's **argument** is his or her opinion on a topic. Arguments are often made in advertisements, editorials, letters, essays, and speeches.

A persuasive essay starts with an introduction. An **introduction** is the first paragraph of an essay in which the main idea is presented. An introduction includes a **topic sentence**, a sentence that gives the main idea of an essay or paragraph, and some general information that is expanded on later in the essay.

When writing an argument, give a clear statement of your position, topic, or point of view. Use language that is appropriate for your audience. Give evidence or examples that will support your position. You might even use emotional language that appeals to people's feelings. In many arguments, the writer will acknowledge the claims of the opposing side and give reasons why those claims are incorrect or unreasonable. A formal writing style is often most appropriate for making an argument.

An argument can be organized by cause and effect, compare and contrast, or problem and solution. Based on your text structure, you should include transition words or phrases. A **transition** is a shift from one idea to the next. Your word choice can help you make smooth transitions between ideas and concepts being discussed. Common transitions found in an argument include *first of all, for example, I feel, in my opinion, on the one hand,* and *on the other hand*.

Read a student's argument below for who should be named Teacher of the Year.

> In my opinion, Ms. Nolan, my science teacher, has the qualities that make a good role model. First of all, she is sincere and wants to help her students to gain an interest in science. She is also aware. She understands that some students have trouble grasping the subject matter, so she works to make the material interesting and clear. Ms. Nolan schedules extra office hours after school so students can figure out where and why they made errors. Also, Ms. Nolan has a terrific sense of humor, so her class always includes a good dose of fun. One time I was frustrated and confused about the homework, and Ms. Nolan cracked a joke that made me laugh so hard I cried.

An argument ends with a concluding section or statement. A **conclusion** recaps the main idea of the whole essay and supports the information presented.

> Because Ms. Nolan is sincere and helpful and is aware of her students' needs, she truly deserves to be named Teacher of the Year.

Organizing your thoughts with a **graphic organizer** can help you include all the points you want to make in your writing. A graphic organizer can help you list evidence or data that will make your argument stronger.

Look at the graphic organizer below. It gives reasons why one student thinks Ms. Nolan should be awarded the title Teacher of the Year.

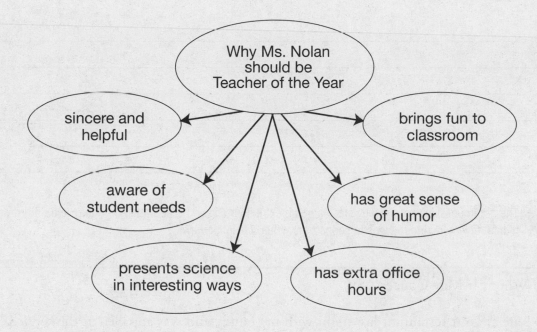

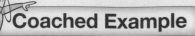

Coached Example

Read the following letters. Then rewrite each one so that the reasons and details support the author's argument.

1. Dear Mom and Dad,

    I think I should be allowed to stay up an extra hour on Friday and Saturday nights. If you let me do it, I'll be so happy. I will even agree to walk the dog an extra time each day so that you don't have to do it.

_____

_____

_____

_____

_____

HINT The argument does not list why staying up an extra hour should be permitted on Friday and Saturday nights. Give concrete reasons to support the writer's point of view.

2. To Whom It May Concern,

    I ate at your restaurant last night with my family and was appalled at the service. It was the worst meal I ever had. And the food tasted terrible, too. Please make some improvements so that people can enjoy going there!

_____

_____

_____

_____

_____

HINT What exactly was wrong with the meal? Give specific reasons and examples to explain why the author was not satisfied with the service and food.

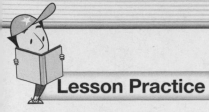

Lesson Practice

Use the Writing Guide to help you understand the passage.

Writing Guide

The author starts by stating a clear topic and a point of view.

Specific reasons are given to support the author's argument.

Is the style and vocabulary correct for the audience and purpose?

Save Woodmere Pond

Littering in Woodmere Pond should be punishable with a large fine. Every time I have been to the pond this week, I have seen trash floating on the top of the water. It is too much to bear!

I think a sign should be posted that lists the fine, and the police should periodically patrol the pond to keep an eye on people who are there.

It should be clear to people why a pond should not be treated like a trash can, but I will try to explain this as clearly as possible. Litter and pollution harm living things. The plants and animals in the pond are being robbed of their natural habitat when humans interfere with the pond. Beverages that spill out of trash bottles seep into the water. This pollutes the water and interferes with the oxygen levels and clarity of the water. Not only does it harm living things, their life cycles, and their food chains, but it is an eyesore in our community. I should not have to go see such an ugly sight when I go to the park.

If the threat of losing money is the only thing that will get people to think about their actions, then a steep fine should be put in place to prevent this kind of behavior.

Which words or phrases from the passage give specific details that support the author's argument?

_____

_____

_____

_____

_____

_____

_____

_____

Plan Your Writing

Read the writing prompt, and then plan your response below.

Think about a rule or law that you would like to pass. First organize your argument in the graphic organizer below. List reasons and details to support your point of view. Tell why you think the law would be a good idea. Then use the next page to write your argument.

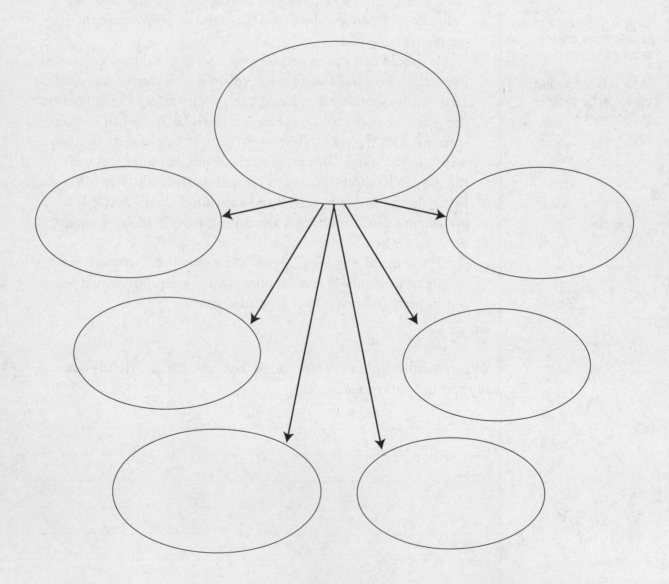

Write Your Response

Write your response in the space provided. You may use your own paper if you need more space.

16 Writing Informative Texts

W.6.2, W.6.10, WHST.6.2, WHST.6.10

Getting the Idea

An **informative text** presents and explains information. Informative texts include newspaper articles, research reports, travel guides, and how-to articles.

When you write an informative text, you should clearly introduce your topic, and develop it with relevant facts and details. **Research** is an investigation of facts and details about a topic. An author can use books, interviews, or online sources to conduct research. Some informative texts use graphics, such as charts and tables, and headings to separate the work into sections. All of these features help the reader to comprehend the text.

An informative text can be organized by sequence, cause and effect, compare and contrast, or problem and solution. Based on your text structure, you should include transition words or phrases. A **transition** is a shift from one idea to the next. Common transitions in an informative text include *another, as a result, due to, first, however, later,* and *unlike*. Your word choice can help you make smooth transitions between ideas and concepts being discussed. When writing an informative text, you should use a formal language style. You also should not include personal opinions.

Read the following text about Hatshepsut, a female ruler of ancient Egypt. Notice that the language is formal, and only facts are given.

> Hatshepsut was one of the few female rulers of ancient Egypt. She was a princess and the wife of the pharaoh, or king. When her husband died, her ten-year-old stepson was supposed to become pharaoh. Hatshepsut said that he was too young to rule on his own. She was named coruler. She ruled for about fifteen years, until her death in 1458 BCE.

An informative text ends with a concluding section or statement. A **conclusion** recaps the main idea of the whole essay and supports the information presented.

> Ancient Egypt did not have many female rules, but Hatshepsut was one of them.

A graphic organizer can help you collect the information for your text. The graphic organizer below shows how the writer collected his thoughts before writing the paragraph about Hatshepsut. The writer decided to use a cause-and-effect pattern that tells what happens as a result of an earlier event.

CAUSE	EFFECT
Hatshepsut's husband was an Egyptian pharaoh.	Hatshepsut was an Egyptian princess.
Hatshepsut's husband died.	Hatshepsut's ten-year-old son became pharaoh.
Boy was too young to rule.	Hatshepsut was named co-ruler.

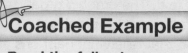

Coached Example

Read the following paragraphs. Then rewrite each one so that they include more concrete details and relevant facts. Research the topics as needed to include the additional information.

1. Because of the unique way in which they are constructed, suspension bridges are the longest kinds of bridges in the world. San Francisco's Golden Gate Bridge is an example of a suspension bridge.

    _____
    _____
    _____
    _____
    _____

    HINT There are no details about how a suspension bridge is made and what makes it different from other kinds of bridges.

2. Pablo Picasso was one of the most influential artists of all time. He was one of the artists credited with the invention of the art movement called Cubism. Today, just a single Picasso painting sells for millions of dollars.

    _____
    _____
    _____
    _____
    _____

    HINT The reader needs more information to get a good sense of who Pablo Picasso was. When did he live? What is Cubism? These details will make the writing more complete.

Lesson Practice

Use the Writing Guide to help you understand the passage.

Writing **Guide**

The topic is introduced at the beginning of the passage.

What transition words do you see? How do they help you identify the text structure?

The author uses precise language to give specific details.

Irrigation Around the World

In some places, such as Egypt or the Arabian Peninsula, it hardly ever rains. From early times, farmers in these places had to find ways to water their crops. In ancient times, people carried river water in buckets to irrigate crops. Because it was such hard work, and because they could not carry enough water to irrigate large fields, they began using machines, such as levers, to help them carry water. This made their chores a lot easier. This method of irrigating crops is called "flood irrigation." However, with flood irrigation a lot of water never gets to the crops, which results in wasted water.

A more modern way of irrigating is by spraying water onto the fields. But dry, windy weather can cause a lot of water to evaporate. In Israel, the climate is very dry. Because there is so little water, the farmers needed to find an efficient way to irrigate crops for growing food. In the 1960s, people there invented "drip irrigation." Pipes with tiny holes in them were laid on the ground, and water flowing through the pipes provided the plant roots with a slow, steady amount of water.

What kinds of graphics might the author want to add to help make the information clearer for the reader?

_____

_____

_____

_____

_____

_____

_____

_____

_____

Plan Your Writing

Read the writing prompt, and then plan your response below.

Throughout history, inventions have helped our society develop. Choose an invention to research and fill in the cause-and-effect chart below to show how that invention has helped society. Include relevant facts and concrete details about the topic. Then use the next page to write your informational text.

CAUSE	EFFECT

Write Your Response

Write your response in the space provided. You may use your own paper if you need more space.

17 Writing Narratives

W.6.3, W.6.10, WHST.6.10

Getting the Idea

A **narrative text** tells a story. Fictional pieces such as novels, short stories, poems, and plays can be narrative texts. Nonfiction pieces such as biographies and autobiographies can be narrative texts.

Narrative texts include characters, a setting, a plot, and a conflict or problem that needs to be resolved. Good narratives have a beginning, middle, and end. Descriptions of the characters and dialogue between characters help make the story more effective.

When organizing a narrative, it helps to follow the plot in order from beginning to end. Stay focused on your main idea or theme. Details and vivid language will help the reader imagine the story's setting. Describe each character's personalities, thoughts, feelings, or appearance.

The paragraph below is an example of narrative writing.

> I was simply frightened out of my skin when I arrived at summer camp that first morning. I had never stayed away from home before, and I wasn't exactly looking forward to the experience. But it was sink or swim for us campers, literally. I met Lori, Carla, and June on the way to rowing class. Our teacher put us together in one boat, and we did our best to stay afloat. That is, until we flipped over and landed right in the lake! About six camp counselors came diving, swimming, and boating to our rescue. I know it sounds strange, but their rescue made me feel a bit comfortable and at home at the camp. I felt like I was going to be safe with the counselors. They really cared about us kids!

The author establishes the setting right away—summer camp. The conflict is that the narrator has never been away from home before and was not looking forward to the summer camp experience. When the narrator and her new friends fall into the lake, the counselors come to their aid immediately. This makes the narrator feel comfortable about the camp. By the end, the narrator feels she will now enjoy the rest of summer camp.

Filling out a graphic organizer can help you plan your narrative. The best kind of graphic organizer to use for narrative writing is a sequence chart. Look at the graphic organizer below. It was filled in by the author of the narrative about summer camp.

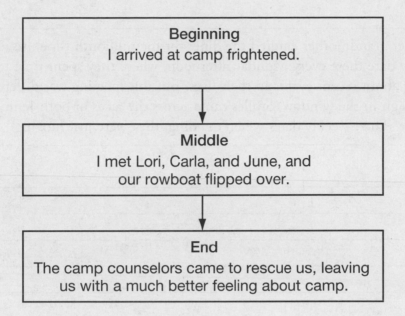

Coached Example

Read the following narratives. Then add sentences that would improve the narratives.

1. Jenny and her grandmother entered the diner for the millionth time, it seemed. They had a weekly date there every Monday afternoon, where they spent time together talking and giggling about recent events in their lives. But this meeting was different. The diner had a huge sign in the window. Smiles came across the faces of both Jenny and her grandmother. Their weekly dates weren't ending, they were just moving!

_____

_____

_____

_____

_____

HINT   There is no apparent conflict in the passage. Also, the author does not tell you what the sign says.

2. Leon knew he would be the star of the concert tonight. He had started playing the piano years before any of the other students. His sister had told him he was being arrogant for thinking he was better than the other students, but Leon didn't care. He continued to think he was above the other students, and he didn't even practice for the performance.

_____

_____

_____

_____

_____

HINT   The story is missing an ending. What happens on the day of the concert? Was Leon correct in his assumption about his piano playing?

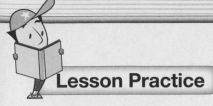

Lesson Practice

Use the Writing Guide to help you understand the passage.

Writing **Guide**

Who is the main character?

What is the setting?

What is the conflict of the narrative?

How does the setting change in the middle of the story?

Mike's Strange Day

Mike's day was awful and getting worse by the minute. His alarm went off late, his clothes were still in the washer, and his jeans were stained with grass.

Mike signed in late at the office and went to PE class. Today was the beginning of basketball. Mike was good at basketball... most days. But today, all he remembered was getting hit on the back of the head by a rebound. He hit the floor...face first.

Suddenly Mike was standing in the shadow of an Egyptian pyramid. He felt a rope slide across his shoulder and almost fell forward. He realized he was part of a crew moving stones up the slope. Mike's day had gone from bad to worse. Throughout the long afternoon, Mike worked to carry boulders.

"Mike, Mike!" He heard the voices, but they sounded so far away. "Mike, can you hear me?"

He opened his eyes. The coach and several classmates were standing around him.

"You just passed out. The school nurse is on the way. How are you feeling?" asked the coach.

"I'm fine; just glad I don't have to carry those boulders anymore."

The group looked at him in wonder, but Mike knew his day could have been a lot worse!

Why do you think Mike thought he was carrying boulders in ancient Egypt?

_____

_____

_____

_____

_____

_____

Plan Your Writing

Read the writing prompt, and then plan your response below.

The story "Mike's Strange Day" explains a day in Mike's life. Choose a day in your life to write about. Use the graphic organizer below to organize the events in your day that you would like to write about. Think about other characters and a conflict you experienced. Then write your narrative on the next page.

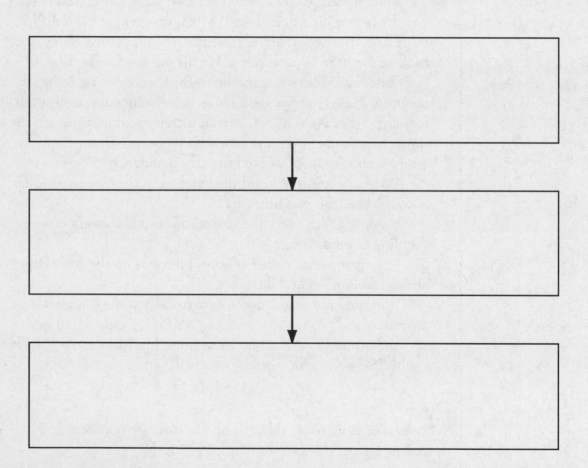

Write Your Response

Write your response in the space provided. You may use your own paper if you need more space.

_____
_____
_____
_____
_____
_____
_____
_____
_____
_____
_____
_____
_____
_____
_____
_____
_____
_____
_____
_____
_____
_____
_____
_____
_____
_____
_____
_____
_____

18 Revising, Editing, and Publishing

W.6.4, W.6.5, W.6.6, WHST.6.4, WHST.6.5, WHST.6.6, L.6.3.a–b, L.6.6

Getting the Idea

There are several steps to the writing process. The first step is to plan your writing. After planning your writing, the next step is to write a draft. A **draft** is a first attempt at writing, which may include errors in organization, content, and mechanics. After you finish your draft, you revise and edit it.

Revising is the process in which writers review what they have written to be sure it is clear, effective, and well organized.

Editing is the process in which mistakes are corrected to ensure the writing follows standard English conventions. A writer will revise and edit his or her work so that it is ready for the publishing stage. He or she should add transitional words or phrases, such as *in addition, furthermore,* and *as a result,* to make the ideas flow better.

Publishing means sharing a finished work with others.

Clear and coherent writing develops ideas, organizes facts and details, and uses appropriate word choices for the audience. Sometimes this kind of clear writing cannot be accomplished the first time the writer makes a draft. It may take a few revisions to get the language and information across clearly and efficiently with the appropriate style and tone.

Sometimes writers review each other's work and give each other guidance and support when editing and making revisions. Teachers also help students develop their writing and maintain a consistent style and tone.

Here are some things good writers look for when revising and editing their work.

What to Look For	What It Means	Bad Example	Good Example
consistent style and tone	The use of the same kind of language and tone throughout a passage, such as formal or informal language.	The trumpet has been a respected instrument in the brass family for centuries. *Toot, toot,* play it!	The trumpet has been a respected instrument in the brass family for centuries. Its vibrant sound is easy to recognize.
precise vocabulary	The use of specific words rather than general ones to convey your ideas.	This drink is good.	This apple cider is delicious.
sentence clarity	Sentences need to be clear and easy to understand. Avoid using too many words.	The thing they thought they were going to do they ended up not doing, even though they would do it.	They didn't do what they thought they were going to do.
sentence order	Sentences should appear in the order that makes the most sense, often starting with a clear topic sentence.	It grows to no more than 40 inches tall. The Shetland pony is a very small breed of horse.	The Shetland pony is a very small breed of horse. It grows to no more than 40 inches tall.
sentence variety	Make your sentences look different. Try not to start two or more sentences the same way, and do not use the same word too many times.	Dean went to look for them in the library. Then Dean went to look for them in the gym.	Dean went to look for them in the library. Then he checked the gym.

Thinking It Through

Read the following paragraph, and then answer the question that follows.

(1) Plants adapt to their habitat, or where they live. (2) For example, burdock plants create seeds with sticky hooks. (3) The hooks cling to the fur of animals that carry the seeds to other places. (4) An adaptation is a body part or feature that helps living things survive under certain conditions. (5) The stem of the cactus plant has a hollow barrel shape that can store water. (6) This is important to life in the desert. (7) The cactus is also covered with long, sharp thorns to keep animals away. (8) Some animals, like the snowshoe hare, use skin or fur coloring to protect themselves. (9) The hare's white fur makes it hard for other animals to see it in the snow. (10) Color adaptations can also warn people and animals to keep away. (11) The bright color of certain animals, such as some snakes, can signal that they are poisonous.

How can you rewrite the beginning of the paragraph so that it starts with a clear topic sentence?

_____

_____

_____

_____

HINT   Is there a topic sentence in the paragraph as it is written now? Where should the topic sentence go?

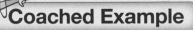

Coached Example

Read the passage and answer the questions.

Hanna had a lot of things to do last week. Hanna had to study for a math test. Hanna had to go to a doctor's appointment. Hanna had to buy a birthday present for her sister. Hanna had to babysit for her baby cousin, too. Hanna was busy but didn't want to miss out on her school activities, either. Hanna had baseball practice on Monday and a school play on Tuesday.

1. How can the author revise the passage to improve it?

   A. Do not repeat the name Hanna so many times.

   B. List fewer things that Hanna has to do.

   C. Add more characters to the story.

   D. Rearrange the sentences in a clearer order.

   HINT Which answer choice tells about something that would make the passage easier to read?

2. What can the author add to tell the reader more about Hanna?

   A. What does Hanna have planned for next week?

   B. How does Hanna feel about her plans?

   C. What will Hanna's school play be about?

   D. What time does Hanna have to babysit her cousin?

   HINT Which answer choice asks a question that tells most about the character?

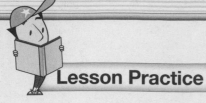

Lesson Practice

This passage contains mistakes. Use the Reading Guide to help you find the mistakes.

Reading Guide

Think about the sentence order and word choice. Does it sound clear and concise?

How can the author revise the last paragraph before publishing the passage?

Teri Returns

(1) Teri walked into the gym and tried not to notice the sudden silence that her entrance had caused. (2) Her teammates had been practicing their routines. (3) Now they all turned to look at Teri. (4) Their faces showed surprise, pity, and delight. (5) They ran to her and took turns hugging her warmly. (6) It had been two weeks since Teri had been at the gym.

(7) "It's so great to see you!" Desiree exclaimed. (8) "How are you feeling?" Maria asked. (9) On any other day, Teri would have enjoyed the attention. (10) Today it was almost too much to bear. (11) Still, it was better than having everyone act as if nothing had happened. (12) Ms. Gill, the team's coach, walked up to the group, and Teri's teammates went back to their routines. (13) Ms. Gill had been a gymnast in high school, too.

(14) "Are you ready?" she asked, searching Teri's face for doubt or fear.

(15) Teri looked over Ms. Gill's shoulder at the balance beam. (16) Two weeks ago, while performing a back walkover she had done a hundred times before, she suffered a bad fall. (17) They took her to Hillcrest hospital.

(18) "I'm ready," Teri answered, and walked over to the balance beam. (19) Feeling everyone's eyes on her, Teri lifted herself onto the beam and walked across it several times to build her confidence. (20) Before she spent too much time thinking about it, she did her walkover. (21) It was perfect.

Answer the following questions.

1. Which transitional word or phrase should be added to the beginning of sentence 10?

   A. As a result

   B. In addition

   C. However

   D. Finally

2. What is the BEST way to improve the organization of paragraph 2?

   A. Leave out sentence 13.

   B. Leave out sentence 12.

   C. Switch sentences 6 and 7.

   D. Move sentence 13 to the beginning of the paragraph.

3. Which sentence would work well as an introductory sentence?

   A. sentence 2

   B. sentence 4

   C. sentence 6

   D. sentence 8

4. Read sentence 17 below.

   They took her to Hillcrest hospital.

   Which change would make the sentence clearer?

   A. Change *her* to *she*.

   B. Change *They* to *Ms. Gill and her teammates*.

   C. Change *took* to *had taken*.

   D. Change *to* to *near*.

5. Why do you think the author does not tell you right away why Teri had not been to the gym in two weeks?

   _____

   _____

   _____

   _____

19 Research and Resources

W.6.7, W.6.8, WHST.6.7, WHST.6.8

Getting the Idea

Research means to gather information about a topic. In nonfiction writing, research is an important stage. A **resource** is something that can be used to help you research a topic. Print resources such as encyclopedias, nonfiction books, and articles in magazines, newspapers, and journals can help. Online resources include trusted Web sites and electronic databases. Make sure the sources you use are current and reliable. The chart below lists and describes common resources that many people use to write reports.

Resource	What It Is
almanac	Book of facts published each year, with lists of important events that occurred that year. It also has current facts and figures on many subjects, from sports to currency exchange.
atlas	Book of maps dealing with a particular country, state, or region. There are also atlases of the entire world.
encyclopedia	Alphabetical listings of topics with a short, factual article on each. Can be one long book or a series of books.
Internet	Network of online resources such as dictionaries, library catalogs, and Web sites. Educational sites, which end in *.edu*, are generally good to use. Look for sites that are written by experts or reliable groups.
newspaper	Daily or weekly publication with reports on local, national, and international events, as well as opinions and features.
nonfiction book	Book on a specific subject based on facts. Nonfiction books are usually written by experts on the subjects.
periodical	Weekly or monthly publication about a topic. Examples are magazines, academic journals, and newsletters.
textbook	A book containing factual information about one field of study. Often covers many topics in a general way.

When you research a topic and use resources for your report, you must give credit to the source where your information came from. Be sure to include the names of your sources in a **bibliography**, or list of sources used for a report or written project. When quoting from a source, you must use quotation marks and credit the source in a footnote.

> As Smith states in his book, "the table is an underrated invention."[1]
>
> [1]Smith, *Inventions*, page 82.

When you **paraphrase**, you put someone else's words into your own words.

> Original sentence: Many people know the story of George Washington chopping down the cherry tree, but this may only be a tall tale with no basis in fact.
>
> Paraphrased sentence: George Washington probably never chopped down a cherry tree, but the story persists until this day.

Although paraphrased ideas do not need to be put in quotation marks, they do need to be credited in the bibliography.

If you are unsure about the reliability of one of your sources, use a second resource to double-check the information. Then include both resources in your bibliography.

Here are some examples of how to list your sources in your bibliography.

A Book by a Single Author
Strauss, Martha. A Single Guide to Cajun Cooking. Chicago: Blue Garnet, 2003.

A Book by More Than One Author
Jones, Eva and Mike Stewart. A History of Great Inventions. New York: Hansen, 2007.

An Encyclopedia Entry
"Jupiter." Encyclopedia of Earth and Science. 2010.

A Magazine Article
Jackson, Shazia. "Where to Bowl in the City." On the Go. 18 March 2009: 11–14.

Thinking It Through

Read the following paragraph, and then answer the questions that follow.

A pelican is a type of water bird. Its telltale feature is the pouch under its beak. Pelicans also have webbed feet and long, narrow beaks. They eat fish, so they tend to live near large bodies of water. They are commonly found in coastal regions or near rivers, though they do not like polar climates. There are several different species of pelicans, found on every continent besides Antarctica. Fossils show that pelicans have existed for over forty million years.

What kind of resource did this paragraph MOST LIKELY come from? What information would someone need about the resource in order to credit it in a bibliography?

_____

_____

_____

_____

HINT Review what information is needed to credit a source in a bibliography.

Coached Example

Read the passage and answer the questions.

Humans have valued honeybees for thousands of years. Rock paintings from 13,000 B.C.E show people gathering honey from wild beehives. Later, the ancient Egyptians learned how to domesticate, or tame, bees so that they could gather honey whenever they wished. Bees were such a precious resource that jars of honey were placed in many pharaohs' tombs.

Today, beekeeping is a big business in the United States because farmers need bees in order for their crops to grow. This humble insect pollinates almost one-third of all the crops grown in the United States.

---

1. If you needed to find out what an Egyptian pharaoh was, which would be the BEST resource to use?

   A. an atlas

   B. a magazine

   C. an encyclopedia

   D. an almanac

   HINT Which resource contains an alphabetical listing of many different topics?

2. Which would be the BEST resource for finding out more about the life cycle of bees?

   A. an almanac

   B. a newspaper

   C. an atlas

   D. a nonfiction book

   HINT Which resource would most likely contain basic information related to the topic of bees?

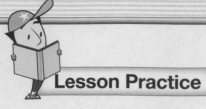

Lesson Practice

Use the Reading Guide to help you understand the passage.

Reading Guide

Which would be the best resources to find more information about King Le Loi?

Which resources would be best to get the most recent information on the Hoan Kiem turtle?

The Hoan Kiem Turtle

In Hanoi, the capital city of Vietnam, people go by the thousands to see turtles in the Hoan Kiem Lake. There are many turtles there, but everyone is hoping to see one very special turtle.

According to legend, over five hundred years ago, King Le Loi defeated the Chinese in battle. He accomplished this with the help of a magic sword that the gods had given him. One day, while he was in a boat on the lake, a giant turtle rose out of the water and informed the king that it was time to return the sword. The king obeyed, throwing it into the lake. He then named the lake "Ho Hoan Kiem," or "Hoan Kiem" for short. This means "Lake of the Returned Sword."

In 1967, a giant turtle was found in the lake. It was about six-and-a-half feet long and weighed over four hundred pounds. The Hoan Kiem turtle proved to be the largest freshwater turtle in the world. When the Hoan Kiem turtle died, its body was preserved. It is now on display on an island in the lake. Some wonder if it is the same giant turtle that took King Le Loi's sword long ago. Others believe that it is a different turtle and that there are other giant turtles in the lake. Other people say that the turtle who took the sword is still in the lake and that it is the only giant turtle that lives there.

Will the mystery of the Hoan Kiem turtle ever be answered? That remains to be seen.

—from the 2001 edition of American Global World Encyclopedia.

Answer the following questions.

1. Which would be the MOST important detail to include in a research paper on the Hoan Kiem turtle?

   A. how many people visit Hoan Kiem Lake every year

   B. how freshwater turtles compare to other turtles

   C. why King Le Loi was fighting the Chinese

   D. the discovery of the giant turtle in 1967

2. Which would be the BEST resource to use to find more information about the Hoan Kiem turtle?

   A. a book about freshwater turtles

   B. a Web site about famous lakes

   C. a magazine article about Hoan Kiem Lake

   D. an article about Hanoi from a travel magazine

3. Which is the correct bibliographic entry for the encyclopedia article "The Hoan Kiem Turtle"?

   A. "Turtle, The Hoan Kiem." American Global World Encyclopedia, 2001.

   B. American Global World Encyclopedia. "The Hoan Kiem Turtle." 2001.

   C. "The Hoan Kiem Turtle." 2001 American Global World Encyclopedia.

   D. "The Hoan Kiem Turtle." American Global World Encyclopedia. 2001.

4. Why must you credit a source you quote or paraphrase?

   A. to let the author of the source gain fame

   B. to let readers know that the ideas are not your original thoughts

   C. to encourage readers to read the original source instead of your own work

   D. to let the author of the source get money for his or her thoughts

5. Why do you think someone doing a report about the Hoan Kiem turtle might need more information than what is provided in this passage?

   _____

   _____

   _____

Cumulative Assessment for Lessons 15–19

This passage contains mistakes. Read the passage and answer the questions that follow.

My Favorite Valentine

(1) Nine out of ten people think I'm completely out of my mind on Valentine's Day. (2) Keep in mind I said *people*, not pets. (3) It's the day when everyone tells the people they love how much they appreciate them. (4) My favorite "person" is my dog, Lincoln. (5) But I can't help it. (6) I really don't like cats all that much.

(7) Lincoln has been in my family since as long as I can remember. (8) I barely remember being a puppy at all. (9) I think we may have been born at the same time, or maybe he was born when I was just two years old. (10) Regarding his age, he is a true friend to me and always has been. (11) Every day when I get off the school bus, he is looking out the living room window to make sure I am coming up the path. (12) Then he attacks me at the door with licks. (13) He rolls over so I can pet his belly, and then we run to the backyard and play together. (14) We have both come to expect this routine every day after school.

(15) So every year when we all choose our valentines and decide who we want to give a special surprise to, I never have trouble deciding who I want my special valentine to be. (16) Lincoln is my one and only valentine. (17) That's why I give him treats on this special day. (18) I give him dog treats that he normally needs to beg for and I wrap them up like presents. (19) He doesn't have to beg today. (20) He can just open them and eat them.

(21) A good dog should also be rewarded with extra playtime on a special day. (22) That's why I'm going to bring Lincoln to the park instead of just the backyard today. (23) The park has a dog run where he can meet other dogs and play as much as he wants. (24) When he is done playing in the park, I will put his leash on and run around the walking trails with him. (25) I can't think of a better way to tell Lincoln that he's my favorite person!

(26) I think my mother will support me when I decide to make Lincoln my favorite valentine. (27) All I really have to do is buy Mom some chocolate, and she will be happy. (28) She knows that Lincoln and I are best friends. (29) That's why I always choose him as my valentine.

1. Where would sentence 2 be better placed?

   A. before sentence 1

   B. after sentence 3

   C. after sentence 4

   D. after sentence 5

2. Which sentence is off-topic and should be removed from the passage?

   A. sentence 4

   B. sentence 6

   C. sentence 21

   D. sentence 26

3. How can the writer improve sentence 15?

   A. Make the sentence longer by adding unnecessary information.

   B. Break the information into two sentences.

   C. Leave the information out of the story.

   D. Add more information and characters to the sentence.

4. Which is the topic sentence of paragraph 5?

   A. sentence 26

   B. sentence 27

   C. sentence 28

   D. sentence 29

5. Read this sentence from the passage.

He can just open them and eat them.

How can the sentence be improved so that it uses better and more descriptive word choices?

A. He can eat them if he wants to.

B. He can open them with a scissor and eat them with a fork.

C. He can just rip them open with his claws and teeth and devour them all day long.

D. He can eat them up and gobble on them.

6. Read this sentence from the passage.

I barely remember being a puppy at all.

Which would be the BEST way to edit the sentence?

A. I barely remember him being a puppy at all.

B. I barely remember a puppy at all.

C. I barely remember him at all.

D. I barely remember him being at all.

7. Read this sentence from the passage.

Regarding his age, he is a true friend to me and always has been.

What is the BEST way to rewrite the sentence for clarity?

A. Regarding his age, he has always been a true friend.

B. Regarding his age, he is really old.

C. Regardless of his age, he is a true friend to me and always has been.

D. Regardless his age, he always has been.

8. What would be another good way to end the passage when it is edited?

A. Delete the last paragraph.

B. Add more information about what kind of chocolates Mom likes.

C. Write about other valentines the narrator has had.

D. Talk about what other people think of the narrator.

Narrative Prompt

Write a story about what it would be like to travel back in time. What would be different from life today? What would be the same? Be sure to include characters, a setting, and a plot in your story, as well as specific details to make your story interesting.

Use the checklist below to help you do your best writing.

Does your story

❏ have a situation and characters?

❏ use dialogue and description to develop the story?

❏ have a clear plot?

❏ use good word choice?

❏ have a satisfying ending?

❏ have good spelling, capitalization, and punctuation?

❏ follow the rules for good grammar and usage?

Write your response on the next page. Use the space below to organize your information in a graphic organizer.

CHAPTER

4 Language

Chapter 4: Diagnostic Assessment for Lessons 20–24

Chapter 4: Cumulative Assessment for Lessons 20–24

Diagnostic Assessment for Lessons 20–24

This passage contains mistakes. Read the passage and answer the questions that follow.

Athena and Arachne

(1) Athena, the greek goddess of war, had an unusual birth. (2) One day, her father, Zeus, suffered an extremely painful headache. (3) His complaining about the pain could be heard all over Mount Olympus. (4) To cure the pain, Hephaestus, the god of fire, split open Zeus's skull with an ax. (5) As the skull split apart, Athena, fully dressed in armor and carrying a spear, burst out of her father's head.

(6) All the gods and goddesses who saw the birth were filled with horror and amazement at the same time. (7) Athena soon became Zeus's favorite child. (8) All the other gods on Mount Olympus—were jealous of her. (9) Many of them often warned Zeus that Athena always did what she wanted and refused to listen to reason. (10) Zeus did not care what anyone else on Mount Olympus thought of Athena. (11) To him, she represented everything good in the world. (12) To everyone in Mount Olympus, Athena was best known for her skill in war, and she loved fighting above all else.

(13) However, she had other skills. (14) No one could rival her in homemaking. (15) She created the first potter's wheel, she made it with it made beautiful vases. (16) But she greatest skill was weaving. (17) She was without a doubt, one of the best weavers that ever lived. (18) After she wove a peice of beautiful cloth, she covered it with even more beautiful embriodery. (19) Athena was extremely proud of her skills with loom and needle and displayed her work for all to see. (20) It was this skill that caused a foolish girl in Lydia to meet her fate—(unfortunately). (21) Athena had such confidence in her that she refused to believe that any god (or human) could rival her.

(22) The girl, who was named Arachne, was equally well known for her skills in weaving and embroidery. (23) Although people had warned her about boasting about its skills, Arachne boldly challenged Athena to a contest. (24) Athena was so angered by the challenge that she accepted, and the foolish Arachne began weaving with great skill. (25) She created a tapestry that showed the love of the gods. (26) When she finished, she showed her work to Athena, who examined it carefully. (27) Athena could find no mistake or bad <u>stitch</u> in the work. (28) She was so angry that a human could weave as skillfully as she that she decided that Arachne must be punished.

(29) Now Arachne was sorry her had ever challenged Athena. (30) Athena changed Arachne into a spider, who was condemned always to spin with threads pulled from her own body. (31) Even today, if you look carefully, you can see Arachne's children spinning their webs in the garden.

1. What is the correct way to rewrite sentence 1?

   A. Athena, the Greek goddess of War, had an unusual birth.

   B. Athena, the Greek Goddess of War, had an unusual birth.

   C. Athena, the Greek goddess of war, had an unusual birth.

   D. Athena, the greek goddess of War, had an unusual birth.

2. Which word from the passage is spelled incorrectly?

   A. warned

   B. peice

   C. skillfully

   D. examined

3. What is the correct way to write sentence 20?

   A. It was this skill that caused a foolish girl in Lydia to meet her fate unfortunately.

   B. It was this skill that caused a foolish girl in Lydia to meet her fate, unfortunately.

   C. It was this skill that caused a foolish girl in Lydia to meet her fate—unfortunately—.

   D. It was this skill that caused a foolish girl in Lydia to meet her fate (unfortunately).

4. As used in sentence 27, stitch means

   A. laughter.

   B. a mend, or fix, of a rip.

   C. a loop of thread.

   D. a sharp pain in the side of the body.

5. What is the correct way to write sentence 21 with an intensive pronoun?

   A. Athena had such confidence in her that they refused to believe that any god (or human) could rival her.

   B. Athena had such confidence in her that she refused to believe that any god (or human) could rival herself.

   C. Athena had such confidence in herself that she refused to believe that any god (or human) could rival her.

   D. Athena had such confidence in herself that she refused to believe that any god (or human) could rival herself.

6. What is the correct way to rewrite sentence 23?

   A. Although people had warned herself about boasting about its skills, Arachne boldly challenged Athena to a contest.

   B. Although people had warned her about boasting about her skills, Arachne boldly challenged Athena to a contest.

   C. Although people had warned him about boasting about its skills, Arachne boldly challenged Athena to a contest.

   D. Although people had warned him about boasting about his skills, Arachne boldly challenged Athena to a contest.

7. What is the correct way to rewrite sentence 16?

    A. But his greatest skill was weaving.

    B. But she greatest skill were weaving.

    C. But her greatest skill was weaving.

    D. But she greatest skill herself was weaving.

8. What is the correct way to rewrite sentence 29?

    A. Now Arachne was sorry him had ever challenged Athena.

    B. Now Arachne was sorry they had ever challenged Athena.

    C. Now Arachne was sorry them had ever challenged Athena.

    D. Now Arachne was sorry she had ever challenged Athena.

9. Which word that means *spider* has a root related to a name in the passage?

    A. archery

    B. arithmetic

    C. arachnid

    D. arcade

10. What is the correct way to rewrite sentence 8?

    A. All the other—gods on Mount Olympus—were jealous of her.

    B. All the other gods on—Mount Olympus—were jealous of her.

    C. All the other gods on Mount Olympus were—jealous of her.

    D. All the other gods on Mount Olympus were jealous of her.

11. Read this sentence from the passage.

Athena changed Arachne into a spider, who was condemned always to spin with threads pulled from her own body.

Rewrite the sentence so that the words have the same denotation, but no longer have a negative connotation.

_____

_____

_____

_____

12. Read this sentence from the passage.

She created the first potter's wheel, she made it with it made beautiful vases.

Rewrite the sentence so that it has no errors.

_____

_____

_____

_____

20 Pronouns

L.6.1.a–d

Getting the Idea

A **pronoun** is a word used in place of a noun. A pronoun can be used as a subject of a sentence or an object of a sentence.

A **subject pronoun** takes the place of the subject in a sentence. The subject pronouns are listed below.

> I   you   he   she   it   we   they
>
> He likes to play chess.

An **object pronoun** takes the place of an object in a sentence. The object pronouns are listed below.

> me   you   him   her   it   us   them
>
> Grandpa played twenty questions with us.

An **antecedent** is the word that a pronoun refers to. Pronouns should always agree with their antecedents in number, person, and gender.

The following shows how to write a sentence with agreement in number.

> The Wilsons had a difficult journey.
>
> *Incorrect:* It had a difficult journey.
>
> *Correct:* They had a difficult journey.

The following shows how to write a sentence with agreement in gender.

> Esther Forbes loved history as a child.
>
> *Incorrect:* He loved history as a child.
>
> *Correct:* She loved history as a child.

The following shows how to write a sentence with agreement in person.

> *Incorrect:* If you want to read the novel, he can get it at our library.
>
> *Correct:* If you want to read the novel, you can get it at our library.

Thinking It Through 1

Read the following sentences. Write them correctly on the lines provided. If the sentence is correct, write "correct as is."

1. He wants to be the first student to finish her test.

_____

HINT What is the subject of the sentence? What is the gender of the subject?

2. Jake and me begged our teacher for a longer recess.

_____

HINT Which pronouns are used to replace the subject of a sentence?

3. Janie brought some lunch down to the lake for Mom and me.

_____

4. Will you please give that book back to my brother and she?

_____

5. I won't answer Jackson's question until he raises he hand.

_____

6. If you want to see the play, he must arrive early.

_____

7. When Maxine and I ran in the race, it wore our favorite sneakers.

_____

8. She and he are my best friends.

_____

A **possessive pronoun** shows ownership. A possessive pronoun can be used alone, or it can be used to describe a noun.

These possessive pronouns can be used alone.

mine   yours   his   hers   ours   theirs

Those gloves are <u>mine</u>.

These possessive pronouns can be used to modify a noun.

my   your   her   his   its   our   their

<u>My</u> pen is on the table.

An **intensive pronoun** emphasizes a noun or pronoun. It takes the place of the antecedent in a sentence so that the same word does not have to be repeated. The following words are intensive pronouns.

myself   yourself   herself   himself   itself
ourselves   yourselves   themselves

The cat amused <u>itself</u> by chasing its tail.

A **vague pronoun** is one that has no clear reference to a noun it replaces.

Jenny was happy with her grades. <u>It</u> made her brother jealous.

The pronoun *it* does not refer back to the nouns *Jenny* or *grades*. It refers to the whole idea that Jenny was happy. You can fix vague pronouns by writing the sentence in different ways.

The fact that Jenny was happy with her grades made her brother jealous.

Jenny's brother was jealous because Jenny was happy with her grades.

Thinking It Through 2

Read the following sentences. Write them correctly on the lines provided. If the sentence is correct, write "correct as is."

1. Please give me back mine umbrella when you are finished with it.

_____

HINT Which possessive pronouns are used alone, and which are used to modify nouns?

2. You are my best friend. It makes me so happy!

_____

HINT Review different ways to fix vague pronouns.

3. Let's go to their house after the movie.

_____

4. The wind made a scary noise through the trees. That was spooky.

_____

5. The girls will have to answer the questions themselves.

_____

6. I bought myselves a cute new pair of shoes.

_____

7. Don't think about taking the train today. It won't work.

_____

8. I think his problems will work itself out.

_____

Lesson Practice

This passage contains mistakes. Use the Reading Guide to help you find the mistakes.

Reading Guide

What does the pronoun *their* refer to in sentence 2?

What is the antecedent for the pronoun *it* in sentence 3?

What is the antecedent for the pronoun *they* in sentence 4?

Book Report on *Treasure Island*

(1) *Treasure Island* by Robert Louis Stevenson is about a young boy named Jim Hawkins. (2) When Jim's father dies, Jim and her mother find a treasure map in the belongings of an old pirate staying at their inn.

(3) Some friends of Jim hire a ship and crew to sail it, including a one-legged man named Long John Silver. (4) Taking Jim along on the voyage, they set off to see if the map leads to treasure. (5) Jim likes Silver until he overhears that Silver and some of the crew are planning to steal the ship once they find treasure.

(6) Of course the plan never happens because Captain Smollett hisself finds out about it. (7) The first of many small battles occur. (8) With every character suspicious of the others, the action gets complicated. (9) Captain Smollett suspects poor Jim. (10) He is taken captive by one side and then escapes.

(11) Throughout the story, you kept wondering if Jim will be able to resist Long John Silver, who is friendly and almost likable. (12) But I kept hoping that Jim would not be too confused because it would end in disaster.

(13) Even though I do not usually enjoy pirate stories, I think *Treasure Island* is a really good book. (14) If someone likes history, action, and adventure, <u>they</u> will definitely enjoy Stevenson's tale.

Answer the following questions.

1. What is the correct way to write sentence 2?

   A. When Jim's father dies, Jim and her mother find a treasure map in the belongings of an old pirate staying at whose inn.

   B. When Jim's father dies, Jim and their mother find a treasure map in the belongings of an old pirate staying at their inn.

   C. When Jim's father dies, Jim and his mother find a treasure map in the belongings of an old pirate staying at their inn.

   D. When Jim's father dies, Jim and his mother find a treasure map in the belongings of an old pirate staying at its inn.

2. Which pronoun should replace the word <u>they</u> in sentence 14?

   A. their

   B. we

   C. he or she

   D. his or her

3. What is the correct way to write sentence 6?

   A. Of course the plan never happens because Captain Smollett himself finds out about it.

   B. Of course the plan never happens because Captain Smollett himselves finds out about it.

   C. Of course the plan never happens because Captain Smollett themself finds out about it.

   D. Of course the plan never happens because Captain Smollett itself finds out about it.

4. What is a better way to write sentence 12?

   A. But I kept hoping that Jim would not end their relationship in disaster and confusion.

   B. But I kept hoping that Jim would not be too confused because surely their relationship would end in disaster.

   C. But I kept hoping that because surely disaster would come of the situation, Jim would not be too confused by the situation.

   D. But I kept hoping that Jim would not be too confused because surely disaster would come of him.

21 Capitalization, Spelling, and Punctuation

L.6.2.a–b

Getting the Idea

Capitalization is the use of uppercase letters in writing. Uppercase, or capital, letters are used to start a sentence. They are also used to start proper nouns and the pronoun *I*. The chart below gives examples of words that require capitalization.

Type of Proper Noun	Examples
book and story titles	*A Wrinkle in Time*, "The Legend of Sleepy Hollow"
days and months	Monday, Sunday, January, October
events or periods	Great Depression, World War II
holidays	Independence Day, Thanksgiving
names of companies	ABC Technology, Fountain Books
names of monuments and buildings	Statue of Liberty, White House, Lincoln Memorial, Stanford Library, Shaker High School
names of people	Jorge, Luanne, Gregory, Maggie
names of places	Main Street, Atlantic Ocean, Chicago
titles of people	Mr., Mrs., Dr., President, Queen

Spelling is the accepted arrangement of letters in words. The chart below lists some commonly misspelled words.

Word	Reason
acceptable, changeable	People tend to end these words in *-ible*, but the *-able* ending is correct.
accommodate, committed	The double *m* is often forgotten in these words, which already have double letters.
foreign, leisure	These words do not follow the *i* before *e* rule.
independent, apparent	People tend to use *-ant* at the end of these words, but the *-ent* ending is correct.
judgment, argument	People often forget to remove the *e* at the end of these root words before the suffix is added.

Thinking It Through 1

Read the following sentences. Write them correctly on the lines provided. If the sentence is correct, write "correct as is."

1. When Mr. conway heard our arguement, he laughed at us.

_____

HINT Review the rules of capitalization of proper names and titles, as well as common spelling rules.

2. Gerry and Sam do the best maintenence work at four corners Garage.

_____

HINT How are names of companies capitalized? Think about how suffixes are added to base words.

3. Should we see that foriegn film called *camilla and jacques*?

_____

4. I think it is acceptable to ask Mr. Lewis to drive us to school.

_____

5. The memorial day parade ocasionally starts a little late.

_____

6. Who was your next door nieghbor on greene street?

_____

7. After walking through the park by himself, Jake felt very independent.

_____

8. Do you think the crack in the liberty bell is noticible?

_____

Punctuation helps readers understand sentences. Each mark of punctuation has a role to play in the sentence. Punctuation tells the reader when ideas begin and end, and when to pause. The chart below shows common punctuation marks and how they are used.

Punctuation	How It Is Used	Examples
comma (,)	Separates words in a series, sets off words of dialogue, or before a conjunction.	Mom said, "Our flag is red, white, and blue, so leave those crayon colors out for the children."
dash (—)	Replaces commas or parentheses in more informal writing to set off phrases or indicate pauses. Use two dashes if the phrase is in the middle of a sentence, and one if it is at the end.	My best friend—Sam—is sick today. Everyone was laughing at him—except me.
exclamation point (!)	Ends sentences that express emotion.	That was an earthquake!
parentheses ( )	Encloses a word, phrase, or sentence that is not essential to the sentence. A sentence or paragraph must be grammatically complete without the phrase in parentheses.	There's no way to get that door open (without breaking the lock), so we'd better call for help.
period (.)	Ends declarative and imperative sentences and is used after abbreviations.	Mr. Woo read a book about America.
question mark (?)	Ends sentences that ask questions.	Who is that?
quotation marks (" ")	Encloses the exact words of a speaker.	Carlos said, "I have an idea."

Thinking It Through 2

Read the following sentences. Write them correctly on the lines provided. If the sentence is correct, write "correct as is."

1. Lori said "You have to clean the dishes before we eat dessert.

_____

> **HINT** Review the rules of commas and quotation marks.

2. There were so many people at your fundraiser—good for you—!

_____

> **HINT** How many dashes are used to set off a phrase that comes at the end of a sentence?

3. We wanted to buy mom a (present) with our money.

_____

4. We can borrow the chairs, tables, and plates for the party.

_____

5. I have seen a lot of interesting (people since) I got here.

_____

6. "Please stand over there" said Jimmy (who was becoming) angry.

_____

7. Whenever anyone asks me that question—anyone, I start to laugh.

_____

8. This is the best (and funniest) show on television.

_____

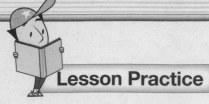

Lesson Practice

This passage contains mistakes. Use the Reading Guide to help you find the mistakes.

Reading Guide

Remember to capitalize names, titles, and the first word in a sentence.

Parentheses indicate an afterthought.

Sometimes there are exceptions to spelling rules.

Douglas "Wrong Way" Corrigan

(1) Douglas Corrigan is one of the most famous aviators in history. (2) He is not famous for doing something right. (3) In fact, he is famous for supposedly making a huge blunder.

(4) When Charles Lindbergh was preparing to fly across the Atlantic Ocean, Corrigan was one of the men who helped build his plane. (5) When Lindbergh succeeded, Corrigan decided that he wanted to fly across the Atlantic someday, too.

(6) He dreamed of flying to ireland, the home of his ancestors. (7) Unfortunately, he could not get permission to make the flight. (8) The government said his plane was not sturdy enough. (9) However, he was certified for a cross-country flight. (10) So in 1938, he took off from New York with a flight plan that would take him to California. (11) Instead of going west, he went east. (12) About 28 hours later he landed in Ireland! (13) He claims that "he got mixed up in the clouds." (14) The government didn't beleive him—but they had no proof he was lying. (15) No real harm had been done, and people enjoyed the humor of the situation.

(16) When he returned home—he was greeted as a hero. (17) They even gave him a ticker-tape parade! (18) Today, the term "Wrong Way Corrigan" is used for people who get mixed up and do the wrong thing.

Answer the following questions.

1. Which part of sentence 6 needs a capital letter?

   A. He dreamed of

   B. flying to ireland

   C. the home

   D. of his ancestors

2. What is the correct way to write sentence 13?

   A. He claims that, "he got mixed up in the clouds."

   B. He claims, "that he got mixed up in the clouds."

   C. He claims that he got mixed up in the clouds.

   D. He claims, that he got mixed up in the clouds.

3. What is the correct way to write sentence 16?

   A. When he returned home (he was greeted as a hero).

   B. When he returned home—he was greeted as a hero—.

   C. When he returned, home, he was greeted as a hero.

   D. When he returned home, he was greeted as a hero.

4. Which of the following phrases from the passage has a misspelled word?

   A. for supposedly making

   B. didn't beleive him

   C. of the situation

   D. could not get permission

22 Multiple-Meaning Words and Roots

L.6.4.a–b, L.6.5.b

Getting the Idea

A **multiple-meaning word** is a word that has more than one definition. To understand which meaning the author intends, use **context clues**, or other words in the same sentence or paragraph. The part of speech of the word in the sentence is also a clue to the meaning of the word. Read the following sentence.

> For Ralph, autumn was the perfect season to take nature hikes.

The word *season* can mean "to add flavoring to food." The word *autumn*, however, points the reader in a different direction. The word is also used as a noun in the sentence. In this sentence, *season* means "a time of year."

There are several context clues that can help you determine the meaning of a multiple-meaning word. The relationships of the other words in the sentence can help. These include cause and effect, part to whole, and item/category.

> Because Sara got low grades on both her spelling and math tests, she was downtrodden.

Based on the cause-and-effect relationship of how someone usually feels when he or she gets low grades, you can determine that the word *downtrodden* means "sad."

A **homonym** is a word that is spelled the same as another word but has a different meaning. A **homograph** is a type of homonym that is spelled the same as another word but has a different meaning and pronunciation. The chart below shows some homonyms.

Word	Meaning 1	Meaning 2
drop	to fall	to stop doing something
fine	well, good	a penalty owed in money
object	a thing, purpose, or goal	to be against
place	an area	to put something somewhere
rich	wealthy	strong, as in flavor or smell
state	area within a country	to say something
turn	to change something different	to move to face in a particular direction

A **root** is a word part that gives a word its main meaning. Many words we use in English come from Greek or Latin roots. An **affix** is the beginning or ending of a word that can change the meaning of a root word. The chart below shows some common roots, their meanings, and how they are used.

Root	Meaning	Examples
alter	other	alternate, alteration
audio	of or related to sound	audience, auditory
grate	pleasing	gratify, grateful
jud	to judge, or decide	judicial, judge
liter	letter	literature, illiterate, literal
mar	of the sea	marine, mariner, maritime
min	small	minute, miniscule, minority
mut	to change	mutate, mutant
photo	of or related to light	photography, photocopy, photojournalism
vic, vinc	to defeat	victorious, invincible

In these examples, the root stays the same, but the affixes can change to change the meaning of each word. An *audience*, for example, is "a group of people who hear a performance." *Auditory* means "related to the sense of hearing." *Audible* means "able to be heard." If you know the meaning of a root, you can figure out the meaning of the word with its affix.

Thinking It Through

Read the following passage, and then answer the question that follows.

On Hector's 11th birthday, he was given a really nice watch from his uncle. It was the watch he had wanted ever since he had seen it in a catalog months before. But, to Hector's surprise, there was something wrong with his brand-new present. He discovered a crack on the glass of the watch's face. The company would have to exchange it for a new one.

Hector knew he must be patient until the new watch came. When the package finally arrived, he couldn't wait to open it. As he untied the bow, Hector knew that the watch would be perfect this time. He took the watch out of the box and smiled from ear to ear. Hector had just received the coolest watch in town!

How can you tell which meaning of the word *patient* the author is writing about? Give examples of the context clues that tell you.

_____

_____

_____

_____

HINT   Look at other words in the sentence to help you.

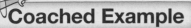

Coached Example

Read the passage and answer the questions.

Philip stared gloomily at the computer screen and sighed. His book report was due tomorrow, yet he was still on the first paragraph. Ms. Chen had given the class two weeks to write the paper, but Philip had kept putting it off. He had played basketball, watched TV, surfed the Internet—anything to avoid writing the report. Finally, a couple of hours ago, he decided to drop everything and sit down at his desk. His <u>object</u> was to finish his paper. Philip glanced at the clock on the wall. The <u>audible</u> ticking of the clock reminded him of his deadline. Philip looked down at the keyboard. He wished this paper could write itself.

1. What does the root of the word <u>audible</u> mean?

   A. awful

   B. able

   C. related to sound

   D. related to clocks

   HINT Use the rest of the sentence and paragraph to help you find the meaning of the root.

2. What is the meaning of the word <u>object</u> in the passage?

   A. goal

   B. to be against

   C. a noun affected by a verb

   D. something that can be touched

   HINT Philip is trying to accomplish something.

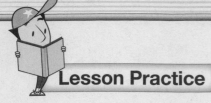

Lesson Practice

Use the Reading Guide to help you understand the passage.

Reading Guide

What is another meaning of the word *coin*?

Find as many homonyms as you can. These are words with more than one meaning.

What is the meaning of *deal*?

Coin Collecting

Some people collect coins for fun, and some collect them for business. Whatever the reason, the rewards of coin collecting can make it a <u>gratifying</u> experience. The value of a coin is determined by how rare it is and its condition. For example, a quarter could be worth far more than twenty-five cents if it is a very rare quarter in <u>mint</u> condition. In contrast, if a quarter is of substandard quality, all it will buy you is a stick of chewing <u>gum</u>.

Collectors have various ways of storing their coins. Some keep their coins in a box. Others buy special books with coin slots. As their collections grow, they often find themselves looking for a very specific coin. That missing piece in a collection can be hard to find. Collectors may spend years trying in vain to find a penny from a particular series in a particular year.

Fortunately, there are many places to buy and sell coins, including coin shops and the Internet. Collectors should do meticulous research before spending big <u>bucks</u> on a coin, however. They should check to see how much the coin is really worth and whether the coin dealer has a good reputation. Some coin dealers are not honest. They will do unethical things like offer to sell the same coin to several buyers and then run off with the money *and* the coin. Some collectors attend coin <u>shows</u>, where dozens of dealers put their coins on display. It is a great way to comparison shop and to get a superb <u>deal</u>.

Answer the following questions.

1. Which meaning of the word <u>mint</u> does the author use in the paragraph 1?

   A. a strong smelling plant

   B. a flavored candy

   C. excellent

   D. a place where money is made

2. Read this sentence from the passage.

   In contrast, if a quarter is of substandard quality, all it will buy you is a stick of chewing gum.

   Which words in the sentence tell you the correct meaning of <u>gum</u>?

   A. In contrast

   B. if a quarter

   C. substandard quality

   D. pack of chewing

3. How do the context clues in paragraph 3 tell you the correct meaning of <u>bucks</u>?

   A. The paragraph is about buying and selling things.

   B. The paragraph is about types of deer.

   C. The paragraph is about how horses can jump.

   D. The paragraph is about collections of things.

4. Which word has the same root as <u>gratifying</u>?

   A. satisfying

   B. gratitude

   C. gravelly

   D. magnifying

5. The last paragraph talks about coin shows. Explain how you know which meaning of <u>shows</u> the author intended.

   _____

   _____

   _____

   _____

   _____

23 Denotation and Connotation

L.6.4.c–d, L.6.5.c

Getting the Idea

A word can have two different kinds of meanings—its dictionary meaning and its implied meaning. The **denotation** of a word is its dictionary meaning. The **connotation** is the implied meaning. A word's connotation is made up of the feelings, memories, or images that come to mind when you hear the word.

For example, the words *house* and *home* have the same general definition, or denotation. They both mean "a place where someone lives." However, many people associate things such as comfort, love, and family with the word *home*. The word *home* has a positive connotation. The word *hovel* is also a synonym for home, but it has a negative connotation. It connotes a lower level of quality. People prefer to live in a house, but not a hovel. The word *house* has a neutral connotation, meaning it is neither positive nor negative.

The word *thrifty* can have a positive connotation. But its synonym, *cheap*, usually has a negative connotation. Similarly, *proud* has a positive connotation, but its synonym, *conceited*, has a negative connotation.

Use a dictionary or a glossary to find the denotation of a word. Below is a sample dictionary entry for the word *young*.

> **young** *adj.* **1.** Being in the early or undeveloped period of life or growth. **2.** Newly begun or formed. **3.** Of or relating to youth or early life.

A thesaurus can give you a hint about a word's connotation by listing words that have the same feeling or tone as the one you are looking up. Below is a sample thesaurus entry for the word *young*.

> **young** *adj.* meaning: being between childhood and adulthood
> *synonyms:* adolescent, immature, juvenile, youthful
> *antonyms:* old, elderly, aged, mature, grown-up, adult, full-grown

The chart explains the denotation and connotation of different words.

Word	Denotation	Connotation	Example
frugal	not generous; economical	being careful with resources responsibly	Joy's *frugal* father always had money set aside for a rainy day.
stingy	not generous	unwilling to share	John was so *stingy*, he only gave his brother one potato chip.
car	automobile	average automobile in good working condition	Mark brought his *car* to the mechanic.
jalopy	automobile	automobile that is not in good condition	Jason's *jalopy* broke down on the interstate.
breeze	moving air	refreshing wind	The sea *breeze* on the beach was welcoming.
gale	moving air	destructive, powerful wind	A *gale* tore my flag to pieces.
terrified	afraid, scared	overwhelmed with fear	Lee was *terrified* as he was about to parachute for the first time.
petrified	afraid, scared	paralyzed with fear; unable to act or move	The hiker was *petrified* when he noticed a mountain lion five feet away.
frightened	afraid, scared	lesser degree of fear, lasting for a brief moment	The raccoon *frightened* Rachel when it jumped out of the garbage can.

Thinking It Through

Read the following passage, and then answer the questions that follow.

The front door slammed, and Rosalinda heard a voice call out, "I'm home!" She hurried out into the hallway to greet her father. She was as excited as a five-year-old child on her birthday. Her father was bringing home a computer!

Rosalinda ran to hug her father. "Did you get it?" she asked.

Mr. Ramonov chuckled. "Yes, I got it. The boxes are in my car. Let's go fetch them together."

Rosalinda knew it would be her best birthday ever.

What is the denotation of the word *slammed* in the first sentence? Does the word have a positive or negative connotation in the passage?

_____

_____

_____

_____

HINT Think of synonyms for the word and think about the context of the sentence.

Coached Example

Read the passage and answer the questions.

Jordan skipped down the sidewalk. She could smell the <u>odor</u> of the blooming rose bushes and hear the bluebirds chirping in the trees. Every part of the world seemed to be alive and <u>thriving</u>. Across the street, Mrs. Jimenez tended to her vegetable garden. She glanced up to wave warmly at Jordan. Jordan's friend Lisa ran out of her house to greet her. They were going to play in Lisa's yard. Jordan loved the spring; it was her favorite season.

1. Read the following sentence.

   She could smell the <u>odor</u> of the blooming rose bushes and hear the bluebirds chirping in the trees.

   Which synonym for <u>odor</u> has a positive connotation?

   A. smell

   B. fragrance

   C. stench

   D. stink

    The correct word is used for something that smells nice, such as perfume.

2. What is the denotation of the word <u>thriving</u>?

   A. dying

   B. struggling

   C. blossoming

   D. greeting

   HINT Think about the context of the word. How is the word used?

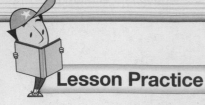

Lesson Practice

Use the Reading Guide to help you understand the passage.

Reading Guide

What are some synonyms for the word *exhausted*?

Think of three synonyms for *thrilled* and decide whether each one has a positive, negative, or neutral connotation.

Which word can you use instead of *scared* to connote the level of Beth's fear?

Stormy Weather

Cold and <u>exhausted</u>, Melissa ran to the car with her homework folder over her head. She knew her homework would be <u>soaked</u>, but she had no choice. The driving rain was too much to avoid. She opened the passenger door as quickly as she could and jumped inside. Then she quickly pulled the door shut.

She had finally made it into the dry car. Melissa didn't want to step foot out of the car again until the rainstorm was completely over. She was drenched but <u>thrilled</u> to be out of the storm and <u>gale</u> outside.

Melissa saw her little sister Beth in the distance, <u>huddled</u> in the doorway with the other kindergartners, waiting to be picked up. Melissa felt a <u>flood</u> of sympathy for her little sister. Beth looked <u>scared</u>, staring out of the school doorway.

"There's an umbrella in the backseat," Melissa's dad told her.

"OK, I'd better go get her," said Melissa. She took a deep breath and hopped out of the car, making a dash for her sister. "Let's go home," she said to her sister as she reached out her hand to her.

Answer the following questions.

1. Read this sentence from the passage.

    She knew her homework would be <u>soaked</u>, but she had no choice.

    Which word with a similar connotation can be used instead of <u>soaked</u>?

    A. wet

    B. drenched

    C. finished

    D. damp

2. What is the denotation of <u>exhausted</u>?

    A. energetic

    B. tired

    C. imagined

    D. feared

3. Read this sentence from the passage.

    Melissa felt a <u>flood</u> of sympathy for her little sister.

    Which word has a similar connotation to <u>flood</u>?

    A. overflow

    B. water

    C. drip

    D. bubble

4. What is the denotation of <u>gale</u>?

    A. car

    B. wetness

    C. strong rain

    D. strong wind

5. How would replacing the word <u>huddled</u> with *cowering* in paragraph 3 change the connotation of the sentence?

    _____

    _____

    _____

    _____

    _____

24 Standard English Usage

L.6.1.e

Getting the Idea

The English language has many rules for writing and speaking correctly. Knowing these rules will help you avoid English language usage errors.

When writing, it is important to write in complete sentences. A **sentence fragment** is an incomplete sentence. It may be missing a subject, or a verb, or a complete thought. A sentence fragment does not make sense on its own because it does not contain an independent clause. An **independent clause** has a subject and verb and expresses a complete thought. Read these examples of sentence fragments.

> After we come back from the library.
> Into the next room.
> Some people who chatted and danced.

To avoid sentence fragments, be sure each of your sentences has a subject, a verb, an independent clause, and end punctuation. Read these examples of correct sentences.

> We have to take a test after we come back from the library.
> I just walked into the next room.
> Some people who chatted and danced missed the dessert.

A **run-on sentence** has two or more independent clauses without correct punctuation to separate them.

> Everyone saw us come in late I was so embarrassed.

You can break run-on sentences into separate sentences so that each one has its own subject. You can also use a conjunction with a comma to make a compound sentence. Another way to fix a run-on sentence is to separate the two independent clauses with a semicolon.

> Everyone saw us come in late. I was so embarrassed.
> Everyone saw us come in late, so I was so embarrassed.
> Everyone saw us come in late; I was so embarrassed.

Thinking It Through 1

Read the following sentences. Write them correctly on the lines provided. If the sentence is correct, write "correct as is."

1. There is no one to open the store it does not open until 10:00.

   _____

   HINT Look for the subject of the sentence. There should be only one.

2. Forever unless you do something about it.

   _____

   HINT What is the subject of the sentence? A complete sentence needs a subject and a verb.

3. Show the man your tickets sit by the main entrance.

   _____

4. Start the grill; I can help you.

   _____

5. The best way to answer your queries and concerns.

   _____

6. I told her she was right about that she didn't believe me.

   _____

7. Sufficient practice on the piano will help you play better.

   _____

8. Laughter and good times for everyone.

   _____

Slang is very informal language or phrases that are not usually thought of as part of our regular language. Slang is often acceptable in speaking but not in writing, unless it is part of a character's dialogue. Here are some examples of slang for the word *good*.

groovy   phat   radical   cool

A **double negative** is the use of two negative statements in the same sentence or clause so that they cancel each other and create a positive statement. The chart below shows how the meaning of a sentence changes with a double negative.

Sentence	Meaning	How to Fix It
She didn't see nothing.	She saw something	She didn't see anything. OR She saw nothing.
I don't have none.	I have some.	I don't have any. OR I have none.

Usage errors are errors in grammar. Use of the correct verb tense, word choice, and verb form are important. Below are some common mistakes in English usage.

Common Usage Errors

Error	Incorrect	Correct
Using the past tense instead of the past participle	I should have went.	I should have gone.
Using a participle instead of a verb tense	I been out of school all week.	I have been out of school all week. OR I was out of school all week.
Confusing adjectives with adverbs	I feel good.	I feel well.
Using unacceptable words	We ain't going.	We aren't going.

Thinking It Through 2

Read the following sentences. Write them correctly on the lines provided. If the sentence is correct, write "correct as is."

1. You drew a well picture of the waterfall, dude.

_____

HINT Does the adjective used to describe the picture make sense, and is slang used?

2. I ain't going to no symphony with those students.

_____

HINT How many negative statements are in the sentence? Are they used correctly?

3. She should have went with them.

_____

4. We wanted to tell the kids that they played a radical game today.

_____

5. Lexi didn't see no people waiting at the bus stop.

_____

6. I don't feel well today, so I'm going to relax at home.

_____

7. There been plenty of people to ask about the homework assignment.

_____

8. She wasn't thinking about anybody's feelings when she said that.

_____

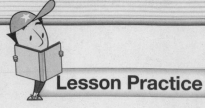

Lesson Practice

This passage contains mistakes. Use the Reading Guide to help you find the mistakes.

Reading Guide

Look for sentence fragments in the passage.

Do you see any double negatives?

If a sentence has more than one independent clause that is not properly connected, the sentence is a run-on sentence.

Gwendolyn the Babysitter

(1) My little sister, Gwendolyn, has her first babysitting job tonight. (2) She has waited for this moment forever she will do just fine. (3) She will only be watching the little boy next door. (4) My parents will only be 50 feet away if she needs them.

(5) Training Gwendolyn for this big day wasn't no easy task. (6) She didn't know anything about caring for a child. (7) It took a while, but I taught her everything I know. (8) Not as knowledgeable as me, of course.

(9) I taught her how to change a diaper, which was the most difficult part of the lessons I gave her. (10) She was patient and listened well, so I knew she wanted to learn. (11) It can definitely be a challenge to take care of a little baby. (12) I showed her how to hold the baby while she was feeding her a bottle.

(13) Gwendolyn owes so much of her knowledge to me, in fact, that I think I should maybe get some of her money! (14) Mom said that was definitely out of the question, so I won't ask again. (15) But if my sis wants to share some of the dough with me, I say yes. (16) I just thought I would let you know.

Answer the following questions.

1. Which is the correct way to write sentence 2?

   A. She has waited for this moment. Forever she will do just fine.

   B. She has waited for this moment forever. She will do just fine.

   C. She has waited for this moment forever she will. Do just fine.

   D. She has waited for this moment forever she will do just fine!

2. Read this sentence from the passage.

   Not as knowledgeable as me, of course.

   How can this sentence fragment be corrected?

   A. She is still not as knowledgeable as me, of course.

   B. Not as knowledgeable as me, of course, as I said.

   C. No one not as knowledgeable as me, of course.

   D. As knowledgeable as me, of course.

3. Read this sentence from the passage.

   But if my sis wants to share some of the dough with me, I say yes.

   How can this sentence be corrected?

   A. But if my sister wants to share the money with me, I be saying yes.

   B. But if my sister wants to share some of the dough with me, I would say yes.

   C. But if my sister wants to share some of the money with me, I would say yes.

   D. But if my sis wants to share some of the money with me, I would say yes.

4. Which sentence from the passage uses a double negative?

   A. She didn't know anything about caring for a child.

   B. It can definitely be a challenge to take care of a little baby.

   C. Mom said that was definitely out of the question, so I won't ask again.

   D. Training Gwendolyn for this big day wasn't no easy task.

Cumulative Assessment for Lessons 20–24

This passage contains mistakes. Read the passage and answer the questions that follow.

The Adventures of Akna

(1) Young Akna, an Inuit boy who lived in the Arctic, loved to go ice fishing on the frozen waters near their home. (2) However, he always had to be on the lookout for thin ice, especially during the warm season when everything melted.

(3) One day as the warm season approached, Akna informed his mother that he was going fishing. (4) "I shall bring home plenty of fish for supper," he said proudly.

(5) "You must be careful of polar bears!" his mother exclaimed worriedly. (6) "I want you to stay safe, Akna!"

(7) Akna remembered that long ago, when he was just an infant, he father had been badly injured by a polar bear during a hunting expedition. (8) But what were the chances that the exact same thing would happen to Akna as had happened to his Father? (9) Akna thought his was invincible. (10) He was young and fast. (11) He would be able to outrun any enemy if faced with that challenge. (12) He was not afraid of polar bears or any other danger on the lake (including thin ice. (13) He had been to the lake a thousand times. (14) "I'll be just fine, Mother!" he said as he ran off toward the lake.

(15) Akna picked up a large rock near some animal tracks, then strolled out to his normal fishing spot. (16) He smashed the heavy rock against the ice to make a hole. (17) Suddenly he, heard a terrible growling sound. (18) He looked up and before him stood the largest polar bear he had ever seen!

(19) Akna was defenseless, and there wasn't nowhere to run. (20) He remembered his mother's words and began to wonder why he had been so stubborn. (21) Now he had no choice but to get out of this mess alive. (22) He stood very still, and then he had a brilliant idea. (23) He remembered a time when he was trapped on the ice as a little boy. (24) His mother had told him to stay calm and everything would be all right. (25) So he stood as still as possible, but his mind still raced a mile a minute. (26) That's when the idea came to him. (27) He suddenly knew what he must do. (28) He carefully leaned down and picked up a chunk of the broken ice. (29) Then he hurled it at the bear.

(30) The poor creature had not expected the human to defend hisself. (31) Frightened by the sting of the ice, the bear turned and ran off into the forest. (32) Excited and reileved, Akna ran home to tell everyone about his adventure. (33) But he stopped when he heard a loud CRACK. (34) He looked back just in time to see the ice where he had been standing break and sink into the lake! (35) *I guess no one is invincible after all,* thought Akna.

1. What is the correct way to revise sentence 9?

   A. Akna thought her was invincible.

   B. Akna thought he was invincible.

   C. Akna thought she was invincible.

   D. Akna thought I was invincible.

2. What is the correct way to revise sentence 8?

   A. But what were the chances that the Exact same thing would happen to Akna as had happened to his Father?

   B. But what were the chances that the exact same thing would happen to akna as had happened to his father.

   C. But what were the chances that the exact same thing would happen to Akna as had happened to his father?

   D. but what were the chances that the exact same thing would happen to akna as had happened to his father?

3. What is the correct way to revise sentence 12?

   A. He was not afraid of polar bears or any other danger on the lake (including thin ice).

   B. He was not afraid of polar bears or any other danger on the lake including thin ice).

   C. He was not afraid of polar bears or any other danger (on the lake including thin ice).

   D. He was not afraid of polar bears or any other (danger on the lake including thin ice).

4. What is the meaning of the word *season* as it is used in sentence 2?

   A. to add herbs or spices to food

   B. a time of the year

   C. something added for flavor

   D. a day of the month

5. What is the correct way to rewrite sentence 30?

   A. The poor creature had not expected the human to defend herself.

   B. The poor creature had not expected the human to defend himself.

   C. The poor creature had not expected the human to defend him.

   D. The poor creature had not expected the human to defend itself.

6. Which word from the passage is spelled incorrectly?

   A. exclaimed

   B. defenseless

   C. relieved

   D. frightened

7. What is the correct way to revise sentence 7?

   A. change *he was just an infant* to *his was just an infant*

   B. change *he was just an infant* to *him was just an infant*

   C. change *he father* to *his father*

   D. change *he father* to *him father*

8. In which word does the root mean the same as it does in the word *invincible*?

   A. invitation

   B. vicinity

   C. invisible

   D. victory

9. What is the correct way to revise sentence 17?

   A. Suddenly, he heard a terrible growling sound.

   B. Suddenly he heard, a terrible growling sound.

   C. Suddenly he heard a, terrible growling sound.

   D. Suddenly, he heard, a terrible, growling sound.

10. What is the correct way to revise sentence 19?

    A. Akna was defenseless, and there was nowhere to run.

    B. Akna was defenseless, and there ain't nowhere to run.

    C. Akna was defenseless, and there weren't nowhere to run.

    D. Akna was defenseless, and there wasn't not nowhere to run.

11. Reread this sentence from the passage.

    Young Akna, an Inuit boy who lived in the Arctic, loved to go ice fishing on the frozen waters near their home.

    Rewrite the sentence using the correct pronoun-antecedent agreement.

    _____

    _____

    _____

    _____

12. Reread this sentence from the passage.

    Now he had no choice but to get out of this mess alive.

    Rewrite the sentence keeping the same denotation but replacing the word *mess* to connote a more serious level of danger.

    _____

    _____

    _____

    _____

**Crosswalk Coach for the
Common Core State Standards,
English Language Arts, Grade 6**

SUMMATIVE ASSESSMENT
FOR CHAPTERS 1–4

Name: _____

Session 1

Read the passage and answer the questions that follow.

The Charge of the Light Brigade
by Alfred Lord Tennyson

Half a league, half a league,
    Half a league onward,
All in the valley of Death
    Rode the six hundred.
5   "Forward, the Light Brigade!
Charge for the guns!" he said:
Into the valley of Death
    Rode the six hundred.

"Forward, the Light Brigade!"
10 Was there a man dismayed?
Not though the soldier knew
    Someone had blundered:
Theirs not to make reply,
Theirs not to reason why,
15 Theirs but to do and die:
Into the valley of Death
    Rode the six hundred.

Cannon to right of them,
Cannon to left of them,
20 Cannon in front of them
    Volleyed and thundered;
Stormed at with shot and shell,
Boldly they rode and well,
Into the jaws of Death,
25 Into the mouth of Hell
    Rode the six hundred.

Flashed all their sabers bare,
Flashed as they turned in air
Sabering the gunners there,
30 Charging an army, while
    All the world wondered:
Plunged in the battery-smoke
Right through the line they broke;
Cossack and Russian
35 Reeled from the saber-stroke
    Shattered and sundered.
Then they rode back, but not
    Not the six hundred.

Cannon to right of them,
40 Cannon to left of them,
Cannon behind them
    Volleyed and thundered;
Stormed at with shot and shell,
While horse and hero fell,
45 They that had fought so well
Came through the jaws of Death,
Back from the mouth of Hell,
All that was left of them,
    Left of six hundred.

50 When can their glory fade?
O the wild charge they made!
    All the world wondered.
Honor the charge they made!
Honor the Light Brigade,
55   Noble six hundred!

1. What is the theme of the poem?

    A. Honor those who died in battle.

    B. Speak up when you know something is wrong.

    C. Do not fight cannons with sabers.

    D. You win some battles, and you lose some.

2. Read the following lines from the poem.

    Came through the jaws of Death
    Back from the mouth of Hell

    What kind of figurative language is used in these lines?

    A. personification

    B. simile

    C. metaphor

    D. idiom

3. How is the poem organized?

    A. by scene

    B. by stanza

    C. by chapter

    D. by paragraph

4. What is the setting of the poem?

    A. a horse track

    B. a baseball field

    C. a battlefield

    D. a haunted house

5. Which point of view does the poet use?

    A. first-person

    B. second-person

    C. third-person omniscient

    D. third-person limited

6. What is the conflict in the poem?

_____

_____

_____

_____

_____

Defending Fort McHenry

In the early days of the United States, the relationship with Great Britain was tense. Ever since the thirteen colonies fought for their independence from Great Britain in 1776, the relationship with the overseas giant had been strained. Great Britain kept troops in American territory long after the war had ended. Great Britain also supported the Native Americans on the frontier. Finally, the British also did whatever they could to keep the United States from succeeding commercially.

It was Britain's wars with France that began to take the biggest toll on Americans. The United States felt that the seas should be considered neutral areas, but the British felt they had control over the seas. The British made a practice of stopping ships on the seas to look for British sailors who were serving on them. They would often take American sailors from ships and force them to serve with the British. This unfair practice was known as *impressment*, and it became a big problem for Americans.

Americans declared war on Great Britain, in what became known as the War of 1812. The war began on June 18, 1812, and continued until 1815.

One of the most memorable moments in the war occurred at Fort McHenry, in Baltimore, Maryland. The defense of American land became more and more important as the war went on. In 1814, England had completed its war with France by defeating Napoleon and his army. Afterward, Britain focused more on the war with the United States. Attacks were more frequent and more intense. The nation's capital of Washington, D.C., was even burned in the battle.

Fort McHenry was built to replace a Revolutionary War fort. It was five-sided, like a star, and built on a peninsula. This design and location gave soldiers on guard the advantage of seeing the enemy from more angles and getting the enemy caught in crossfire if they came too close to the fort.

About a month after the burning of Washington, D.C., the British began attacking Baltimore. Fort McHenry was under attack. On September 13, special ships called ketches began bombing the shores and the fort. There were more than 1,500 cannons and mortars flung at the fort for twenty-five straight hours. American troops did what they could to defend their fort. Cannons were set up at all areas around the fort. Americans fought back the best they could, but their cannons did not fire as far as the British ships could. The Americans were facing a difficult battle. Twenty-four solders were wounded, and four were killed in the ordeal.

Although the fort was bombarded with cannons and mortar fire, the battle, which became known as the Battle of Baltimore, became a turning point in the war. It was decided that the battle was won by the Americans because, after twenty-five hours of battle, the fort still stood, and the American defenses were strong.

This battle may have gone down in history as one of the many battles of the War of 1812. But the actions of one lawyer changed American attitudes about the war. On the night of the attack, the American lawyer Francis Scott Key was dining aboard a British ship to negotiate the release of some captured American soldiers. When the fighting broke out, he was forced to stay aboard the ship and wait until the battle was over.

Francis Scott Key did more than just wait for the battle to be over, however. He wrote a poem about the battle that inspired Americans. His poem, "Defence of Fort McHenry," celebrated the determination and willful spirit of the Americans who defended the fort. The words of his poem became some of the most patriotic in America's history and eventually became the national anthem known as "The Star-Spangled Banner." You may be most familiar with the first and most famous stanza of the four-stanza poem.

Oh, say can you see by the dawn's early light
What so proudly we hailed at the twilight's last gleaming,
Whose broad stripes and bright stars through the perilous fight
O'er the ramparts we watched were so gallantly streaming?
And the rockets' red glare, the bombs bursting in air,
Gave proof through the night that our flag was still there.
Oh, say does that star-spangled banner yet wave
O'er the land of the free and the home of the brave?

The imagery of the rockets and bombs streaming through the air has become symbolic of American bravery and valor. The idea of the flag still flying, even after a terrible night of battle, has given inspiration to many Americans and has been a reminder to troops who may feel defeated in battle.

Fort McHenry not only survived the twenty-five-hour Battle of Baltimore, but it has survived to this day as an American memorial and attraction for many.

7. Which word from the passage are you MOST LIKELY to find only in texts about social studies or history?

   A. stanza

   B. lawyer

   C. impressment

   D. inspired

8. What kind of graphic would be MOST helpful for people reading this text?

   A. a map of Fort McHenry

   B. a map of Great Britain

   C. a timeline of battles won by American troops

   D. a timeline of battles won by British troops

9. What can you infer about Francis Scott Key from reading the passage?

   A. He had pride in the British government.

   B. He had pride in the United States.

   C. He felt afraid during the Battle of Baltimore.

   D. He was glad that so many people liked his poem.

10. Which resource would you use to find more information about Francis Scott Key?

   A. almanac

   B. atlas

   C. encyclopedia

   D. newspaper

11. Which part of the passage includes the author's opinion?

    A. "The war began on June 18, 1812, and continued until 1815."

    B. "Oh, say can you see by the dawn's early light"

    C. "The idea of the flag still flying, even after a terrible night of battle, has given inspiration to many Americans and has been a reminder to troops who may feel defeated in battle."

    D. "Although the fort was bombarded with cannons and mortar fire, the battle, which became known as the Battle of Baltimore, became a turning point in the war."

12. On the lines below, write a summary of the passage.

    _____

    _____

    _____

    _____

    _____

excerpted from

Major Barbara

by George Bernard Shaw

ACT I

It is after dinner on a January night, in the library in Lady Britomart Undershaft's house in Wilton Crescent. A large and comfortable settee is in the middle of the room, upholstered in dark leather. A person sitting on it (it is vacant at present) would have, on his right, Lady Britomart's writing table, with the lady herself busy at it; a smaller writing table behind him on his left; the door behind him on Lady Britomart's side; and a window with a window seat directly on his left. Near the window is an armchair.

Lady Britomart is a woman of fifty or thereabouts, well dressed and yet careless of her dress, well bred and quite reckless of her breeding, well mannered and yet appallingly outspoken, treated as a naughty child until she grew into a scolding mother, and finally settling down with plenty of practical ability and worldly experience.

Her son, Stephen, comes in. He is a gravely correct young man under twenty-five, taking himself very seriously, but still in some awe of his mother, from childish habit and bachelor shyness rather than from any weakness of character.

STEPHEN: What's the matter?

LADY BRITOMART: Presently, Stephen.

Stephen meekly walks to the settee and sits down. He takes up The Speaker, *a newspaper.*

LADY BRITOMART: Don't begin to read, Stephen. I shall require all your attention.

STEPHEN: It was only while I was waiting—

LADY BRITOMART: Don't make excuses, Stephen. (*He puts down* The Speaker.) Now! (*She finishes her writing; rises; and comes to the settee.*) I have not kept you waiting very long, I think.

STEPHEN: Not at all, mother.

LADY BRITOMART: Bring me my cushion. (*He takes the cushion from the chair at the desk and arranges it for her as she sits down on the settee.*) Sit down. (*He sits down and fingers his tie nervously.*) Don't fiddle with your tie, Stephen: there is nothing the matter with it.

STEPHEN: I beg your pardon. (*He fiddles with his watch chain instead.*)

LADY BRITOMART: Now are you attending to me, Stephen?

STEPHEN: Of course, mother.

LADY BRITOMART: No: it's not of course. I want something much more than your everyday matter-of-course attention. I am going to speak to you very seriously, Stephen. I wish you would let that chain alone.

STEPHEN: (*hastily letting go of the chain*) Have I done anything to annoy you, mother? If so, it was quite unintentional.

LADY BRITOMART: (*astonished*) Nonsense! (*with some remorse*) My poor boy, did you think I was angry with you?

STEPHEN: What is it, then, mother? You are making me very uneasy.

LADY BRITOMART: (*squaring herself at him rather aggressively*) Stephen: may I ask how soon you intend to realize that you are a grown-up man, and that I am only a woman?

STEPHEN: (*amazed*) Only a—

LADY BRITOMART: Don't repeat my words, please: It is a most aggravating habit. You must learn to face life seriously, Stephen. I really cannot bear the whole burden of our family affairs any longer. You must advise me: you must assume the responsibility.

STEPHEN: I!

LADY BRITOMART: Yes, you, of course. You were twenty-four last June. You've been at Harrow and Cambridge. You've been to India and Japan. You must know a lot of things now; unless you have wasted your time most scandalously. Well, advise me.

STEPHEN: (*much perplexed*) You know I have never interfered in the household—

LADY BRITOMART: No: I should think not. I don't want you to order the dinner.

STEPHEN: I mean in our family affairs.

LADY BRITOMART: Well, you must interfere now; for they are getting quite beyond me.

STEPHEN: (*troubled*) I have thought sometimes that perhaps I ought; but really, mother, I know so little about them; and what I do know is so painful—it is so impossible to mention some things to you—(*He stops, ashamed.*)

LADY BRITOMART: I suppose you mean your father.

STEPHEN: (*almost inaudibly*) Yes.

LADY BRITOMART: My dear: we can't go on all our lives not mentioning him. Of course you were quite right not to open the subject until I asked you to; but you are old enough now to be taken into my confidence, and to help me to deal with him about the girls.

STEPHEN: But the girls are all right. They are engaged.

LADY BRITOMART: (*complacently*) Yes: I have made a very good match for Sarah. Charles Lomax will be a millionaire at thirty-five. But that is ten years ahead; and in the meantime his trustees cannot, under the terms of his father's will, allow him more than eight hundred pounds a year.

STEPHEN: But the will says also that if he increases his income by his own efforts, they may double the increase.

LADY BRITOMART: Charles Lomax's exertions are much more likely to decrease his income than to increase it. Sarah will have to find at least another eight hundred pounds a year for the next ten years; and even then they will be as poor as church mice. And what about Barbara? I thought Barbara was going to make the most brilliant career of all of you. And what does she do? Joins the Salvation Army; discharges her maid; lives on a pound a week; and walks in one evening with a professor of Greek whom she has picked up in the street, and who pretends to be a Salvationist, and actually plays the big drum for her in public because he has fallen head over ears in love with her.

STEPHEN: I was certainly rather taken aback when I heard they were engaged. Cusins is a very nice fellow, certainly: nobody would ever guess that he was born in Australia; but—

LADY BRITOMART: Oh, Adolphus Cusins will make a very good husband. After all, nobody can say a word against Greek: it stamps a man at once as an educated gentleman. And my family, thank Heaven, is not a pig-headed Tory one. We are Whigs, and believe in liberty. Let snobbish people say what they please: Barbara shall marry, not the man they like, but the man I like.

13. What kind of character trait BEST describes Stephen?

    A. nervous

    B. kind

    C. daring

    D. tricky

14. Read the following line from the play.

    Sarah will have to find at least another eight hundred pounds a year for the next ten years; and even then they will be as poor as church mice.

    What kind of figurative language is used in this line?

    A. personification

    B. simile

    C. idiom

    D. metaphor

15. How is the text in the passage organized?

    A. by scene

    B. by stanza

    C. by chapter

    D. by paragraph

16. What can you infer about Stephen's relationship with his father?

    A. Stephen and his father had a relationship of mutual respect.

    B. Stephen's father has done things that upset him.

    C. Stephen has never met his father.

    D. Stephen and his father were business partners.

17. Lady Britomart wants Stephen to tend to the family affairs, but Stephen seems reluctant. Which part of the plot is this?

    A. setting

    B. climax

    C. conflict

    D. resolution

18. On the lines below, write a summary of the passage.

_____

_____

_____

_____

_____

Read the passage and answer the questions that follow.

The True Father of Baseball?

When you think about the game of baseball, you might think about giant stadiums packed with fans, or small-town ball fields with packed stands filled with friends and neighbors. The sound of a baseball cracking against a wooden bat, followed by the eruption of cheering fans brings to mind the everyday joys of baseball. For generations the sport has been an American pastime. There is one person in particular we can look back to and thank for making baseball what it is today. That person is A. G. Spalding.

Albert Goodwill Spalding was born in September 1850 in Byron, Illinois. He played baseball as a child and always loved the game. In 1865, he joined his first competitive team, called the Rockford Pioneers. It was during his time with this youth team that he became known for his excellent pitching skills. He was approached by an adult team called the Forest Citys after he pitched a 26–2 victory over another team. He played for the Forest Citys for two years before accepting a professional contract to play with a team for the pay of $40 a week.

Baseball was a growing sport at that time, and the first professional organization was formed, called the National Association of Professional Base Ball Players (NAPBBP). Spalding began playing for this league on a team called the Boston Red Stockings. He had a great record in this club, winning 205 games as a pitcher, and losing 53. As a hitter he also did a great job, batting a .323 average.

The NAPBBP became known for questionable operations and gambling. The owner of the Chicago White Stockings, William Hulbert, wanted to change all that. He wanted to start a professional baseball league that had a better reputation and was not corrupt. He asked for Spalding's help, and the two men began a new league called the National League of Professional Baseball Clubs, or simply, the National League. This remains one of the two major leagues today.

Spalding was well known in professional baseball. In 1876, he won forty-seven games as a pitcher and led the White Stockings to capture the first-ever National League pennant. He continued with various related business ventures, namely a sporting goods company with his brother in 1877. The company manufactured and sold various sports equipment, including a new piece of equipment called a baseball glove. In his professional games, Spalding began using the glove to catch baseballs. He was the first professional player to do this, and it helped his sporting goods business immensely when other people began looking to buy the glove for themselves. A. G. Spalding & Brothers sold these gloves in their store.

The sporting goods store became one of his most enjoyable and profitable endeavors, and he retired from baseball a year later. While running his sporting goods store, he also served as president of the Chicago White Stockings from 1882 to 1891.

A. G. Spalding & Brothers had a great influence on the game of baseball. The sporting goods company developed the ball that would become standardized for play and become the official ball in the professional leagues. Before that time, there was no standard in quality for professional baseballs, and this affected the statistics of the players and the quality of the games.

A standardized baseball is made using the following process:

1. Start with a cork or rubber sphere measuring 13/16 of an inch.
2. Encase the sphere in two pieces of black rubber.
3. Join the black rubber pieces together with two red rubber washers.
4. At this point, the center of the ball should be 4 1/8 inches in circumference.
5. Wrap a thread of woolen yarn around the center until the circumference is 7 3/4 inches.
6. Wrap a second layer of woolen yarn around the center until the circumference is 8 3/16 inches.
7. Wrap a third layer of woolen yarn around the center until the circumference is 8 3/4 inches.
8. Wrap a fourth layer of polyester-cotton yarn around the center until the circumference is 9 inches.
9. Cover the yarn with two pieces of cowhide.
10. Measure the circumference; the circumference of the ball must be 9 to 9 1/4 inches.
11. Measure the diameter; the diameter of the ball must be 2 7/8 to 3 inches.
12. Using red thread, double stitch the two pieces of cowhide together 108 times.
13. The ball must weigh between 5 and 5 1/4 ounces.

Spalding's company also published the first official rulebook for baseball. The baseball bats we use today were developed and designed by Albert Spalding's company. In 1911, Spalding published the first scholarly account of baseball's history. It was called *America's National Game* and contains first-hand accounts of the beginnings of America's favorite pastime.

Twenty-five years after the sporting goods company opened, it became a chain and the company continued to grow. Today you can see the name Spalding on countless sports equipment and athletic gear. You'll also see Spalding's name on many soccer balls and golf balls, and in professional basketball.

Albert Spalding had a great love and talent for baseball, but his influence on all of sports can be seen by his accomplishments with his sporting goods company.

19. What is the main idea of the passage?

   A. A. G. Spalding was a better baseball player than a businessman.

   B. A. G. Spalding helped found the National League.

   C. A. G. Spalding played for the first professional baseball league.

   D. A. G. Spalding was an influential person in baseball as well as business.

20. Which text structure does the author MOSTLY use in the passage?

   A. problem and solution

   B. cause and effect

   C. compare and contrast

   D. question and answer

21. What kind of graphic is shown with the passage?

   A. a map

   B. a diagram

   C. a photograph

   D. an illustration

22. Which persuasive technique does the author use to convince the reader that A. G. Spalding was an important influence on baseball?

   A. bandwagon

   B. loaded words

   C. inclusion of facts

   D. avoidance of facts

23. According to the process for making a standard baseball, which step comes after covering the cork with the black and red rubber?

   A. Wrap a thread of wool around the center until the circumference is 7 3/4 inches.

   B. Wrap a second layer of wool around the center until the circumference is 8 3/16 inches.

   C. Cover the yarn or string with two pieces of cowhide.

   D. Using red thread, double stitch the two pieces of cowhide together 108 times.

24. Which resource would you use to look up the number of winning and losing games of a professional ball team last year?

   A. almanac

   B. atlas

   C. encyclopedia

   D. textbook

25. How do you think A. G. Spalding's professional image as a baseball player affected the success of his sporting goods company?

   _____

   _____

   _____

   _____

   _____

Read the passage below and answer the questions that follow.

"Chapter 14: The Islet"

excerpted and adapted from

Kidnapped

by Robert Louis Stevenson

As I stepped ashore, I began the most unhappy part of my adventures. It was half-past twelve in the morning, and though the wind was broken by the land, it was a cold night. I dared not sit down (for I thought I should have frozen), but took off my shoes and walked to and fro upon the sand, barefoot, and beating my breast with great weariness. There was no sound of man or cattle; not a cock crowed, though it was about the hour of their first waking. Only the surf broke outside in the distance, which put me in mind of my perils and those of my friend. To walk by the sea at that hour of the morning—and in a place so desert-like and lonesome—struck me with a kind of fear.

As soon as the day began to break, I put on my shoes and climbed a hill—the toughest scramble I ever undertook—falling, the whole way, between big blocks of granite, or leaping from one to another. When I got to the top, the dawn had come. There was no sign of the ship, which must have lifted from the reef and sunk. The boat, too, was nowhere to be seen. In what I could see of the land, there were no houses or people.

I was afraid to think what had happened to my shipmates, and afraid to look longer at so empty a scene. What with my wet clothes and weariness, and my belly that now began to ache with hunger, I had enough to trouble me without that. So I set off eastward along the south coast, hoping to find a house where I might warm myself, and perhaps get news of those I had lost. And at the worst, I considered the sun would soon rise and dry my clothes.

After a little, my way was stopped by a creek or inlet of the sea, which seemed to run pretty deep into the land. As I had no way to get across, I changed my direction to go about the end of it. It was still the roughest kind of walking; indeed the whole, not only of the town of Earraid, but of the neighboring part of Mull (which they call the Ross) is nothing but a jumble of granite rocks with flowering heather growing among it. At first the creek kept narrowing as I had looked to see; but now to my surprise it began to widen again. At this I scratched my head, but still had no notion of the truth: until at last I came to a rising ground, and it burst upon me all in a moment that I was cast upon a little barren isle, and cut off on every side by the salt seas.

Instead of the sun rising to dry me, it began to rain, with a thick mist; so that my situation was quite bad.

I stood in the rain, and shivered, and wondered what to do, till it occurred to me that perhaps I could walk through the creek. Back I went to the narrowest point and waded in. But not three yards from shore, I plunged in head over ears; and if I lived, it would be by God's grace rather than my own carefulness. I was no wetter (which would not even be possible), but I was much colder after this mishap; and much unhappier after having lost even more hope.

And now, all at once, the yard—the piece of the ship's mast—came in my head. I remembered I left something there that would help me now. With that I bravely set off across the top of the isle, to fetch and carry it back. It was a weary tramp in all ways, and if hope had not encouraged me, I would have thrown myself down and given up. Whether with the sea salt, or because I was growing ill, I was distressed with thirst. I had to stop, as I went, and drink the dirty water out of the hags.

I came to the bay at last, more dead than alive. At first glance, I thought the yard was something farther out than when I left it. I went, for the third time, into the sea. The sand was smooth and firm, and shelved gradually down, so that I could wade out till the water was almost to my neck and the little waves splashed into my face. But at that depth my feet began to leave me, and I dared venture in no farther. As for the yard, I saw it bobbing very quietly some twenty feet beyond.

26. What is the conflict in the passage?

A. The narrator cannot find shoes that fit.

B. The narrator is trying to survive after a shipwreck.

C. The narrator is having trouble navigating a large ship.

D. The narrator cannot remember where he lives.

27. From which point of view is the story told?

A. first-person

B. second-person

C. third-person limited

D. third-person omniscient

28. Read the following sentence from paragraph 3.

> **And at the worst, I considered the sun would soon rise and dry my clothes.**

This sentence foreshadows the moment in the passage when

A. the narrator discovers he is on a barren islet.

B. it starts to rain and the narrator's clothes get wetter.

C. the narrator falls into water that is up to his ears.

D. the narrator stops during his trek to drink dirty water.

29. What effect did wading through the creek have on the main character's journey?

A. He reached the bay.

B. He found a lot of fish to eat.

C. He discovered his shipmates.

D. He found the ship but no shipmates.

30. Why do you think the character refers to this part of the journey as the "most unhappy" part of his adventures?

A. He did not know where he was going.

B. He had to complete it without his friends.

C. It was difficult to describe to other people.

D. It was filled with difficult and dangerous situations.

excerpted and adapted from

The Disappearance of Lady Frances Carfax
by Sir Arthur Conan Doyle

"But why Turkish?" asked Mr. Sherlock Holmes, gazing at my boots. I was reclining in a cane-backed chair at the moment, and my large feet had attracted his ever-active attention.

"The boots are English," I answered in some surprise. "I got them at Latimer's, on Oxford Street."

Holmes smiled with an expression of weary patience.

"No, the bath!" he said. "The bath! Why the relaxing and expensive Turkish bath rather than the invigorating homemade article?"

"Because for the last few days I have been feeling achy and old. A Turkish bath is what we call an alterative in medicine—a fresh starting point, a cleanser of the system.

"By the way, Holmes," I added, "I have no doubt the connection between my boots and a Turkish bath is perfectly self-evident to a logical mind, and yet I should like you to explain it to me."

"The train of reasoning is not very obscure, Watson," said Holmes with a mischievous twinkle. "It belongs to the same simple class of deduction which I should illustrate if I were to ask you who shared your cab this morning."

"A fresh illustration is not really an explanation," said I with some harshness.

"Bravo, Watson! That was a very dignified and logical protest. Let me see, what were the points? Take the last one first—the cab. You observe that you have some splashes on the left sleeve and shoulder of your coat. Had you sat in the center of a horse-drawn carriage you would probably have had no splashes, and if you had, they would certainly have been symmetrical. Therefore it is clear that you sat at the side. Therefore it is equally clear that you had a companion."

"That is very evident."

"Absurdly commonplace, is it not?"

"But the boots and the bath?"

"Equally childish. You are in the habit of lacing up your boots in a certain way. Today, I see them fastened with an elaborate double bow, which is not your usual way of tying them. You have, therefore, had them off. Who has tied them? A boot maker—or the boy at the bath. It is unlikely that it is the boot maker, since your boots are nearly new. Well, what remains? The bath. Absurd, is it not? But, for all that, the Turkish bath has served a purpose."

"What is that?"

"You say that you have had it because you need a change. Let me suggest that you take one. How would Lausanne in Switzerland do, my dear Watson—first-class tickets and all expenses paid on a princely scale?"

"Splendid! But why?"

Holmes leaned back in his armchair and took his notebook from his pocket.

"One of the most dangerous people in the world," said he, "is the drifting and friendless woman. She is the most harmless and often the most useful of people, but she eventually encourages crime in others. She is helpless. She is migratory. She has sufficient means to take her from country to country and from hotel to hotel. She is lost, as often as not, in a maze of obscure pensions and boardinghouses. She is a stray chicken in a world of foxes. When she is gobbled up, she is hardly missed. I much fear that some evil has come to the Lady Frances Carfax."

I was relieved at this sudden descent from the general to the particular. Holmes consulted his notes.

"Lady Frances," he continued, "is the sole survivor of the direct family of the late Earl of Rufton. The estates went, as you may remember, in the male line. She was left with limited means, but with some very remarkable old Spanish jewelry of silver and curiously cut diamonds to which she was fondly attached—too attached, for she refused to leave them with her banker and always carried them around with her. A rather pathetic figure, the Lady Frances is a beautiful woman, still in fresh middle age, and yet, by a strange change, the last person lacking means of support of what was a good family twenty years ago."

"What has happened to her, then?"

"Ah, what has happened to the Lady Frances? Is she alive or dead? There is our problem. She is a lady of precise habits, and for four years it has been her unchanging custom to write every second week to Miss Dobney, her old governess, who has long retired and lives in Camberwell. It is this Miss Dobney who has consulted me. Nearly five weeks have passed without a word. The last letter was from the Hotel National at Lausanne. Lady Frances seems to have left there and given no address. The family is anxious, and as they are exceedingly wealthy no sum will be spared if we can clear the matter up."

31. What evidence in the passage tells the reader that Holmes and Watson are friends?

    A. They are both trying to solve the same crime.

    B. They speak as if they are familiar with each other.

    C. They both have the same opinions.

    D. They both know Lady Frances Carfax.

32. What can you infer about Watson's feelings toward Sherlock Holmes?

    A. Watson is upset that Holmes gets involved with his private matters.

    B. Watson pities Holmes for not having any other companions.

    C. Watson is jealous of Holmes's observational and deduction skills.

    D. Watson gets annoyed and becomes impatient with Holmes's way of talking.

33. From which character's point of view is the story told?

    A. Watson's

    B. Sherlock Holmes's

    C. Lady Frances Carfax's

    D. Arthur Conan Doyle's

34. What is the theme of the passage?

    A. Crime doesn't pay.

    B. Don't trust anyone.

    C. Heroes are important in our lives.

    D. Being observant can be very helpful.

35. Read this sentence from the passage.

    She is a stray chicken in a world of foxes.

    What kind of figurative language is used in this sentence?

    A. personification

    B. idiom

    C. simile

    D. metaphor

36. Explain how "The Disappearance of Lady Frances Carfax" is similar to and different from the excerpt "Chapter 14: The Islet."

_____

_____

_____

_____

_____

_____

_____

_____

Read the passage below and answer the questions that follow.

Gravity and Our Solar System

Gravity is the force that attracts objects toward the center of Earth. When you let go of a book, gravity causes that book to fall to the floor. When you jump up in the air, you feel confident that you will come back down. But what is the science behind gravity? Is gravity on Earth the same throughout the whole solar system? English physicist and mathematician Sir Isaac Newton first described this phenomenon in terms of scientific law in 1687.

The law of gravity spreads far beyond Earth. The entire solar system functions with this force. Not only does gravity hold us to Earth, it also holds all the planets of our solar system and their moons in their orbits around the sun. Without the pull of gravity, the planets, moons, and stars would float off through space. Gravity is a guiding force in our solar system.

As Sir Isaac Newton discovered hundreds of years ago, we can measure the pull of gravity. A Newton is the standard unit of force to measure gravity. Each planet has a different amount of gravity pulling on it. For example, Earth's pull of gravity is 9.81 meters (about 32 feet) per second squared. The chart below shows the percent of gravity that other planets have compared to Earth.

Planet	Distance from the Sun	Gravity Compared to Earth
Mercury	58,000 kilometers	38% of Earth's gravity
Venus	107,000 kilometers	91% of Earth's gravity
Mars	227,000 kilometers	38% of Earth's gravity
Jupiter	774,000 kilometers	254% of Earth's gravity
Saturn	1,419,000 kilometers	108% of Earth's gravity
Uranus	2,856,000 kilometers	91% of Earth's gravity
Neptune	4,475,000 kilometers	119% of Earth's gravity

The laws of gravity are not as clear and simple as one calculation, however. Factors that go into determining the amount of gravity on a planet or a moon include mass—how much matter it contains—and distance. A planet with a lot of mass will have a greater pull of gravity. A planet farther from the sun will have a weaker pull of gravity. That is why the planets listed above do not decrease in gravity's pull based only on their distance from the sun. The more massive planets have a greater pull of gravity.

When a person on Earth weighs 100 pounds, we are talking about the force of attraction between the person and Earth. That same person who weighs 100 pounds on Earth can go to every other planet and every other moon in the solar system and have a different weight. Weight is the amount of mass multiplied by gravity. In fact, a 100-pound person on Earth would weigh 2,707 pounds on the sun! The pull of gravity is much greater there than in other places in the solar system. If that person were able to travel to a very dense star called a white dwarf, he or she would weigh 130 million pounds! On a neutron star, that person would weigh 14 trillion pounds. That's because a neutron star has an extremely small radius and extremely high density. The chart below shows what a 100-pound person would weigh on each of the other planets in our solar system.

Planet	Distance from the Sun	Weight
Mercury	58,000 kilometers	37.8 pounds
Venus	107,000 kilometers	90.7 pounds
Mars	227,000 kilometers	37.7 pounds
Jupiter	774,000 kilometers	236.4 pounds
Saturn	1,419,000 kilometers	106.4 pounds
Uranus	2,856,000 kilometers	88.9 pounds
Neptune	4,475,000 kilometers	112.5 pounds

The same rules apply to a person's weight on each planet's moon. On our moon, a 100-pound person would weigh 16.6 pounds. If that person then traveled to some of the moons of Jupiter, he or she would weigh 18.35 pounds on Io, 13.35 pounds on Europa, 14.48 pounds on Ganymede, and 12.64 pounds on Callisto.

Keep in mind that this 100-pound person would keep the same mass in all of these places in the solar system even though his or her weight will fluctuate considerably in each location. Historic film footage shows American astronauts Neil Armstrong and Buzz Aldrin bouncing along on the moon's surface during their 1969 mission. That's because they were nearing weightlessness on the surface of the moon, at less than 20 percent of their weight on Earth.

37. Why does the author use charts to present information in the passage?

   A. Charts are more accurate than graphs.

   B. Charts provide a visual representation of facts that makes them easier to understand.

   C. Charts give the reader information about a topic different from the passage.

   D. Charts present information in chronological order.

38. Where would a reader look to find the MOST recent information about new discoveries about Jupiter's moons?

   A. atlas

   B. encyclopedia

   C. textbook

   D. Internet

39. To calculate the weight of a human on Venus, a scientist needs to know the person's mass and

   A. the person's weight on Earth.

   B. Venus's gravitational pull.

   C. Venus's atmosphere and climate.

   D. the person's mass on other planets.

40. Which word or words would MOST LIKELY be found only in a scientific text about astronomy?

   A. determining

   B. neutron star

   C. density

   D. radius

41. How is the information presented in the charts in the passage?

    A. by cause and effect

    B. by sequence

    C. by compare and contrast

    D. by problem and solution

42. What will happen to a person's weight if his or her mass increases?

    A. the weight increases

    B. the weight decreases

    C. the weight stays the same

    D. the weight fluctuates up and down

History of the Space Program

People have wondered about space for centuries and have made efforts to explore it. Ever since Galileo Galilei first gazed into space with a telescope, people have wondered how they can get there to see the planets and moons first hand.

When you think about it, the space program has been around for a very short time compared to the amount of time we have spent wondering about space. The United States was not even the first nation to place an object into space. It was the Russians who launched *Sputnik 1*, the first human-made object, to orbit Earth. It was launched on October 4, 1957, and stayed in orbit for three months. In November 1957, *Sputnik 2* orbited Earth for seven days, carrying a dog as a passenger.

These satellites launched by the Russians prompted the United States to increase its efforts to get into space. The competition between the two countries, known as the *space race*, had begun. In 1958, just three months after *Sputnik 1* was launched, the United States placed its own satellite into orbit. *Explorer 1* was launched on January 31, 1958, and it was America's first successful attempt at launching a satellite into orbit around Earth. Afterward, both the United States and Russia (then known as the U.S.S.R.) did their best to further their space programs and exploration of space.

In 1958, the U.S. government created the National Aeronautics and Space Administration (NASA). NASA would be responsible for the U.S. space program and space research. It would train astronauts who would go into space and also collect and analyze information gathered from expeditions into space.

Each new mission to space was a "first" for human space travel. The first satellite to orbit the moon, the first weather satellite in space, and the first spy satellites all brought useful information to scientists. However, it was the U.S.S.R. that sent the first human into space. The *Vostok 1*, carrying Russian cosmonaut Yuri A. Gargarin, orbited Earth once. Just one month later, the United States launched *Freedom 7* into space with U.S. astronaut Alan B. Shepard Jr., though he did not orbit Earth. Astronaut John Glenn Jr. became the first American to orbit Earth on February 20, 1962. He circled Earth three times in the spacecraft called *Friendship 7*.

Even more groundbreaking space flights followed. The first live transatlantic telecast was provided by a U.S. satellite in 1962; the first close-range photos of the moon were taken by *Ranger 7* in 1964; and the first space walk was made by Russian Cosmonaut Alexei A. Leonov in 1965. He floated in space for a total of twelve minutes and gained the attention of the world. Three months later, American astronaut Edward White II made a space walk, this time for twenty-two minutes. Eventually, both nations set their sights on the moon and wanted to be the first to land an astronaut there.

The United States was the first to make this mission a success. On July 20, 1969, Michael Collins, Neil Armstrong, and Edwin "Buzz" Aldrin Jr. took *Apollo 11* to the moon for a successful landing and moonwalk. Since this historic mission, there have been many other missions into space. The U.S. space shuttles have taken astronauts into space for various missions to collect data and explore space.

Today, the space race between the United States and Russia is over, and nations are more willing to work together to expand our knowledge and experience in space. Since 1998, the International Space Station has been under construction. This research facility in space is being developed by many countries, including Russia, Japan, the United States, and Canada. The costs of such an undertaking in space would be too much for one nation to handle alone, and the knowledge gained will benefit more nations at once. So, after so many years of competition, the space race seems to have turned into cooperation in space.

43. Which sentence from the passage reflects the author's opinion?

    A. "Since 1998, the International Space Station has been under construction."

    B. "Each new mission to space was a 'first' for human space travel."

    C. "So, after so many years of competition, the space race seems to have turned into cooperation in space."

    D. "In 1958, the U.S. government created the National Aeronautics and Space Administration (NASA)."

44. Which word from the passage would you MOST LIKELY find in a technical text about the history of the Russian space program?

    A. program

    B. analyze

    C. launching

    D. cosmonaut

45. How much longer after *Sputnik 1* launched did *Sputnik 2* go into orbit?

    A. one month

    B. three months

    C. seven months

    D. one year

46. Where would you MOST LIKELY find the most information about the U.S. space program during the year 1965?

    A. atlas

    B. almanac

    C. dictionary

    D. newsletter

47. What can you infer about the overall mood of the United States and Russian citizens during the space race?

    A. They were upset about how slow the exploration was going.

    B. They were competitive about winning the space race.

    C. They were confused about the technologies being used in space.

    D. They were angry at their governments for exploring space.

48. How are the main idea and topic of "Gravity and Our Solar System" similar to and different from the main idea and topic of "History of the Space Program"?

_____

_____

_____

_____

_____

A Letter from Camp

Dear Mom and Dad,

(1) Please pick me up at summer Camp. (2) This has been the most difficult summer I have ever had here. (3) One of my bunkmates is really annoying. (4) First of all, he snores so loud at night that I can't sleep. (5) So when I have to wake up and go to breakfast at 7:00 in the morning, it's like I haven't slept all night. (6) I feel completely exhausted all day.

(7) Now, I know you'll tell me that I should tell a counselor about my problem and ask to be assigned to a different bunk. (8) The problem is my already did that. (9) They say that everyone must deal with the bunk assignments that they were given. (10) My counselor said that they get about twenty requests every summer from kids who don't like their bunkmates, so they decided not to let anyone at all <u>switch</u>. (11) The food here is actually inedible. (12) He said that if the camp granted everyone their wishes the bunk assignments would be total chaos. (13) So, that leaves me on the losing end of this battle.

(14) And that's not the only problem I have to face every day. (15) It has to be the worst food that has ever been cooked for human consumption. (16) After every meal, at least three kids get sick from the food. (17) It's just terrible.

(18) The kids here are fine, but they are not my friends from home that's for sure. (19) I can deal with the counselors, but I hate that they don't respect my problem with my snoring bunkmate.

(20) The biggest reason I want you to pick me up from camp is that I am unhappy with these other things. (21) Isn't camp supposed to be a fun experience you know that I've loved summer camp for the past four years I have come here. (22) Why should you spend so much money to provide me with an enriching and enjoyable summer experience if it's actually the exact opposite for me? (23) If it was my kid who wrote to me and told me he hated an expensive camp, I'd drive right up there and take him home. (24) Would you? (25) I sure hope you will.

Your loving son,

Adrian

49. Where would sentence 11 be better placed?

   A. after sentence 14

   B. after sentence 9

   C. after sentence 19

   D. after sentence 17

50. What is the correct way to rewrite sentence 8?

   A. The problem is mine already did that.

   B. The problem is me already did that.

   C. The problem is you already did that.

   D. The problem is I already did that.

51. What is the correct way to rewrite sentence 1?

   A. Please pick me up at summer camp.

   B. Please pick Me up at summer camp.

   C. Please pick me up at Summer camp.

   D. Please pick me up at Summer Camp.

52. Read the dictionary entry below.

switch *noun* 1. The bushy tip of an animal's tail. 2. A device for breaking or opening an electrical circuit. *verb*. 3. To shift, transfer, or change. 4. To cause an electrical current to start or cease operation.

Which meaning for <u>switch</u> is used in sentence 10?

   A. definition 1

   B. definition 2

   C. definition 3

   D. definition 4

53. What is the BEST way to rewrite sentence 18?

   A. The kids here are fine—but they are not my friends from home that's for sure.

   B. The kids here are fine, but they are (not) my friends from home that's for sure.

   C. The kids here are fine, but they are not (my friends from home) that's for sure.

   D. The kids here are fine, but they are not my friends from home—that's for sure.

54. Rewrite sentence 15 so that it has a similar denotation, but a more positive connotation.

_____

_____

_____

_____

55. Rewrite sentence 21 so that it is grammatically correct.

_____

_____

_____

_____

STOP

Session 2

Persuasive Prompt

Think about a change you would like to make in your neighborhood. Write a letter to your local newspaper that explains what change you would like to make and convinces others that this would be a good change. Be sure to include the reasons why the change is needed, as well as specific details to make your letter more persuasive.

Use the checklist below to help you do your best writing.

Does your letter

❏ have a clear topic?

❏ show a point of view about that topic?

❏ have a logical structure?

❏ support reasons with details?

❏ connect reasons and details with the right words or phrases?

❏ use a style and vocabulary that is correct for the audience and purpose?

❏ have a solid conclusion?

❏ have good spelling, capitalization, and punctuation?

❏ follow the rules for good grammar?

Write your response on the pages provided. You may use your own paper if you need more space.

Glossary

adventure story a plot with a lot of action in which characters go on a journey (Lesson 6)

affix the beginning or ending of a word that can change the meaning of a root word (Lesson 22)

almanac a book of facts published each year, with lists of important events that occurred that year (Lesson 19)

antecedent the word that a pronoun refers to (Lesson 20)

argument the way a writer tries to convince the reader to think or act in a certain way (Lessons 13, 15)

atlas a book of maps (Lesson 19)

author's purpose the reason an author writes (Lesson 14)

bandwagon a propaganda technique that tries to convince a reader to do something because everyone else is doing it (Lesson 13)

bias a prejudice toward one point of view (Lesson 13)

bibliography a list of sources used for a report or written project (Lesson 19)

book a long story written in sentences and paragraphs and possibly divided into chapters (Lesson 5)

capitalization the use of upper-case letters in writing (Lesson 21)

caption a small amount of text that can help to explain a graphic (Lesson 12)

cause a reason something happens (Lesson 9)

cause and effect a text structure that gives reasons and outcomes for events (Lesson 9)

chapter a division of a book into logical parts (Lesson 5)

character a person, animal, or other creature in a story (Lesson 1)

climax action that helps characters resolve a conflict in a story (Lesson 1)

comma punctuation that separates words in a series, sets off words of dialogue, or before a conjunction (Lesson 21)

compare to tell how two or more texts are alike (Lessons 6, 9, 14)

compare and contrast a text structure that tells how two or more things are alike and different (Lesson 9)

conclusion a section or statement that recaps the main idea of the whole essay and supports the information presented (Lessons 15, 16)

conflict a problem in a story that needs to be solved (Lesson 1)

connotation an implied meaning of a word apart from its dictionary meaning (Lesson 23)

context clues words in the same sentence or paragraph as an unfamiliar word that help readers determine its meaning (Lesson 22)

contrast to tell how two or more texts are different (Lessons 6, 9, 14)

dash punctuation that replaces commas or parentheses in more informal writing to set off phrases or indicate pauses. Use two dashes if the phrase is in the middle of a sentence, and one if it is at the end. (Lesson 21)

denotation the literal meaning of a word (Lesson 23)

diagram a drawing with labels (Lesson 12)

double negative the use of two negative statements in the same sentence or clause so that their meaning is positive (Lesson 24)

draft a first attempt at writing that may include many errors in organization, content, and mechanics (Lesson 18)

drama literature that is meant to be acted out (Lesson 5)

editing a process in which mistakes are corrected to ensure the writing follows standard English conventions (Lesson 18)

effect the result of a cause (Lesson 9)

encyclopedia alphabetical listings of topics with a short, factual article on each; can be one long book or a series of books (Lesson 19)

exclamation point punctuation that ends sentences that express emotion (Lesson 21)

fact a statement that can be proved to be true or false (Lesson 13)

fantasy a story that includes many elements that could not happen in real life and takes place in places that may not exist (Lesson 6)

figurative language language that does not mean exactly what it says (Lesson 4)

first-person point of view when a character tells a story using the pronoun *I* or *we,* and the narrator is a character in the story (Lessons 2, 14)

flashback when the present action in a story pauses to describe an earlier event (Lesson 5)

flowchart a graphic that shows the sequence of events (Lesson 12)

foreshadowing a clue about what is going to happen later in a story (Lesson 5)

genre a kind of writing (Lesson 6)

graphic an image that helps the reader better understand the written information in a passage or text (Lesson 12)

graphic organizer a graphic that helps writers organize their thoughts before writing (Lesson 15)

historical narrative a made-up story set in a real time in the past and that includes characterizations of real people (Lesson 6)

homograph a word that is spelled the same as another word but has a different meaning and pronunciation (Lesson 22)

homonym a word that is spelled and pronounced the same as another word but has a different meaning (Lesson 22)

idiom a saying or phrase that does not mean literally what it says; usually particular to a region or group (Lesson 4)

inclusion or avoidance of facts a propaganda technique in which the writer mentions only facts that will help persuade readers to his or her opinion (Lesson 13)

independent clause a clause with a subject and verb that expresses a complete thought (Lesson 24)

inference an educated guess based on evidence in the text and a reader's prior knowledge (Lesson 7)

informative text a text that presents and explains information (Lesson 16)

intensive pronoun a word that emphasizes a noun or pronoun (Lesson 20)

Internet network of online resources such as dictionaries, library catalogs, and Web sites. Educational sites, which end in *.edu,* are generally good to use. Look for sites that are written by experts or reliable groups. (Lesson 19)

introduction the first paragraph of an essay in which the main idea is presented (Lesson 15)

literal language language that means exactly what it says (Lesson 4)

literary device a technique used to produce a specific effect on a reader (Lesson 5)

loaded language a propaganda technique in which the writer uses language that is more dramatic or emotional than necessary (Lesson 13)

main character the character that a writer focuses on the most (Lesson 1)

main idea the most important idea in a text (Lesson 8)

map a drawing of a location (Lesson 12)

metaphor a comparison that is implied or suggested without using the word *like* or *as* (Lesson 4)

multiple-meaning word a word that has more than one definition (Lesson 22)

multistep instructions text structure that tells a reader how to make or do something (Lesson 10)

mystery a plot in which a puzzle, riddle, or crime must be solved (Lesson 6)

narrative text a text that tells a story (Lesson 17)

narrator the person who tells a story (Lesson 2)

newspaper daily or weekly publication with reports on local, national, and international events, as well as opinions and features (Lesson 19)

nonfiction book book on a specific subject based on facts. Nonfiction books are usually written by experts on the subjects they are about. (Lesson 19)

object pronoun a word that takes the place of the object in a sentence (Lesson 20)

opinion a statement that cannot be proved (Lesson 13)

paraphrase to put someone else's words into your own words (Lesson 19)

parentheses punctuation that encloses a word, phrase, or sentence that serves as an afterthought. A sentence or paragraph must be grammatically complete without the phrase in parentheses. (Lesson 21)

period punctuation that ends declarative and imperative sentences and is used after abbreviations (Lesson 21)

periodical weekly or monthly publication about a topic. Examples are magazines, academic journals, and newsletters. (Lesson 19)

personification giving human qualities to an animal, object, or idea (Lesson 4)

persuasion a way to change how a reader thinks, acts, or feels about something (Lesson 13)

persuasive writing writing that tries to convince the reader of the writer's argument (Lesson 15)

picture a visual representation of what something looks like (Lesson 12)

plot the sequence of events in a story (Lesson 1)

poetry literature written in lines with creative language and often includes rhythm and rhyme (Lesson 5)

point of view the way a narrator tells a story (Lesson 2)

possessive pronoun a word that shows ownership that can be used alone, or can be used to describe a noun (Lesson 20)

primary source a first-hand account of a topic of interest or event (Lesson 14)

problem a difficult situation, obstacle, or challenge (Lesson 9)

problem and solution a text structure where an obstacle or challenge must be overcome or a problem must be solved (Lesson 9)

pronoun a word used in place of a noun (Lesson 20)

propaganda technique a way that a writer can use bias to convince the reader of a certain point of view (Lesson 13)

publishing sharing a finished work with others (Lesson 18)

punctuation marks that help readers understand sentences (Lesson 21)

question mark punctuation that ends sentences that ask questions (Lesson 21)

quotation marks punctuation that encloses the exact words of a speaker (Lesson 21)

research to gather important information about a topic (Lessons 16, 19)

resolution the way a conflict is solved in a story (Lesson 1)

resource something that can be used to help someone research a topic (Lesson 19)

revising the stage when writers review and correct what they have written to be sure it is clear, effective, and well organized (Lesson 18)

root a word part that gives a word its main meaning (Lesson 22)

run-on sentence two or more main clauses without correct punctuation to separate them (Lesson 24)

scene the setting of a play and the place where the story takes place and the characters interact (Lesson 5)

scientific and technical texts texts that include science lessons, scientific experiments, and technical manuals (Lesson 11)

secondary source a document that relates information that is not a primary source (Lesson 14)

second-person point of view when a narrator uses the pronoun *you* to tell a story (Lesson 2)

sentence fragment an incomplete sentence (Lesson 24)

sequence chronological or time order (Lesson 9)

setting the time and place that a story occurs (Lesson 5)

simile a direct comparison of one thing to another using the word *like* or *as* (Lesson 4)

slang very informal language or a phrase that is not usually thought of as part of our regular language (Lesson 24)

solution the answer to a problem (Lesson 9)

spelling the accepted arrangement of letters in words to help with pronunciation (Lesson 21)

stanza a group of lines that make up a verse, or one unit of a poem (Lesson 5)

steps in a process text structure that explains to the reader how to do something (Lesson 10)

subject pronoun a word that takes the place of the subject in a sentence (Lesson 20)

summary a short retelling of a text in the reader's own words (Lessons 3, 8)

supporting detail a fact that describes, explains, or strengthens the main idea of a text (Lesson 8)

table a chart that shows information in columns and rows (Lesson 12)

text structure the way an author chooses to present information (Lessons 5, 9)

textbook contains factual information about one field of study. Often covers many topics in a general way. (Lesson 19)

theme a main message, lesson, or idea in a text (Lesson 3)

third-person limited point of view when a narrator tells the story through the thoughts and feelings of only one character (Lesson 2)

third-person omniscient point of view when a narrator knows everything about a story and its characters (Lesson 2)

third-person point of view when someone outside the story narrates using the pronouns *they*, *he*, or *she* (Lessons 2, 14)

timeline a list of events organized by date (Lesson 12)

topic sentence a sentence that gives the main idea of an essay or paragraph and some general information that is expanded on later in the essay (Lesson 15)

traits qualities that tell the reader about a character (Lesson 1)

transition a word or phrase that helps writers shift from one idea to another (Lessons 15, 16)

usage errors mistakes in grammar or general language (Lesson 24)

vague pronoun a pronoun that has no clear reference to a noun it replaces (Lesson 20)

word choice when an author's choice of words is used to create a particular meaning (Lesson 11)

Mechanics Toolbox

 ## Verb Tense

The **tense** of a verb expresses the time of the action. There are three simple tenses: present, past, and future.

The **present tense** expresses action that is happening now.

> I <u>walk</u> to the post office.
> He <u>eats</u> his breakfast with gusto.
> We <u>know</u> the way home from here.

The **past tense** expresses action that happened at an earlier time, in the past. The past tense of a regular verb such as *walk* is formed by adding the suffix *-ed.* The past tense of irregular verbs such as *eat* and *know* do not follow a pattern and need to be learned.

> I <u>walked</u> to the post office yesterday.
> He <u>ate</u> his breakfast before his morning run.
> We once <u>knew</u> the way home from here.

The **future tense** expresses action that will happen at some later time, in the future. The future tense is formed by using the verb *will* with the main verb.

> I <u>will walk</u> to the post office tomorrow.
> He <u>will eat</u> his breakfast after showering and getting dressed.
> We <u>will know</u> the way home after we study the map.

 ## Maintain a Consistent Style and Tone

The **style** of a piece of writing is the way it is written. For example, a textbook might be written in a clear and plain style. A picture book might be written in a playful style.

The **tone** of a piece of writing shows the way the writer feels about the topic. Compare these examples:

> It really stinks that you're sick. Shake off that cold soon! (informal tone)
> I am sorry to hear about your illness. I hope that you get better soon. (formal tone)

Informal language is everyday language. **Formal language** is spoken or written more carefully. Use formal language when you want to show respect.

Punctuation

The **comma (,)** is used to separate the items in a list.

> The magnolia trees, daffodils, and tulips all bloomed at once.
> Dad cooked the steak, shrimp, and vegetables on the grill.

A **semicolon (;)** may also be used to separate the items in a list if one or more of the items includes a comma.

> The siblings were born on October 8, 2003; August 23, 2006; and May 14, 2009.

The purpose of using semicolons is to avoid confusion. Consider the following example that does not include semicolons:

> To prepare for the party, Elsie wanted to vacuum, wash, dry, and set out the dishes, and put away the magazines that were scattered all over the apartment.

As this sentence is punctuated, it seems that Elsie wants to vacuum her dishes. The correct sentence is:

> To prepare for the party, Elsie wanted to vacuum; wash, dry, and set out the dishes; and put away the magazines that were scattered all over the apartment.

Another use of commas is to set off a parenthetical phrase. A **parenthetical phrase** is a phrase within a sentence that adds to, but is not necessary to, the meaning of a sentence.

> Brian, <u>also a talented pitcher</u>, hit three home runs in Saturday's game.

 ## Pronouns

A **pronoun** is a word that takes the place of a noun. The form of a pronoun shows both person and number.

Person refers to the point of view expressed by the pronoun: first person (the person speaking, or *I*), second person (the person spoken to, or *you*), or third person (the person or thing spoken of, or *he*, *she*, or *it*).

Number refers to how many people or things the pronoun represents. A **singular** pronoun represents one person or thing. A **plural** pronoun represents more than one person or thing.

This chart features the personal pronouns.

	Singular	Plural
First Person	I, me	we, us
Second Person	you	you
Third Person	he, him; she, her; it	they, them

An **antecedent** is the word that a pronoun replaces. Pronouns and antecedents need to agree in person and number. Third-person singular pronouns and antecedents also need to agree in gender.

The antecedent for a pronoun may appear in a previous sentence. It may also appear earlier within the same sentence as the pronoun.

My family travels a lot. We have even been to New Zealand. (correct)
I enjoy scary movies. It's so thrilling! (incorrect)
Whenever Alex and Kate visit the zoo, they go to see the lions first. (correct)
When a person makes a mistake, they should admit it. (incorrect)

In the second example, the singular pronoun, *It*, does not agree with the plural antecedent, *movies*. In the fourth example, the plural pronoun, *they*, does not agree with the singular antecedent, *person*. The correct sentences are:

I enjoy scary movies. They are so thrilling!
When people make mistakes, they should admit it.

It also needs to be clear which noun is the antecedent of a pronoun. Consider this example:

The children brought their toys to the park, and they got very dirty.

The antecedent of *they* is not clear. Did the children get very dirty, or did their toys? If the children got dirty, the pronoun is not necessary. The correct sentence is:

The children brought their toys to the park and got very dirty.

Sentence Structures

A sentence is a group of words that tells a complete thought. It has a subject and a predicate. The **subject** tells who or what the sentence is about. The **predicate** tells what the subject does.

> The crickets chirp.

The crickets is the subject of this sentence. The predicate is *chirp*. It tells what the crickets do.

Joining words called **conjunctions** can be used to combine two or more simple sentences. The common coordinating conjunctions are *and, but, or, nor, for, yet,* and *so.*

> They drove all day to get back home. The sun was setting when they arrived.
> They drove all day to get back home, <u>and</u> the sun was setting when they arrived.

> Roger enjoys playing the piano. He does not like to sing.
> Roger enjoys playing the piano, <u>but</u> he does not like to sing.

Notice that a comma is used before each coordinating conjunction.

Words such as *after, although, because, however, if, until,* and *when* are used as subordinating conjunctions. If a subordinating conjunction is used to combine two sentences, the meaning of one sentence becomes dependent on the other.

> Amelia rides her bicycle to school every day. She could take the bus.
> Amelia rides her bicycle to school every day, <u>although</u> she could take the bus.

A subordinating conjunction can begin a sentence.

> Summer vacation begins at the end of June. We will visit my grandparents.
> <u>When</u> summer vacation begins at the end of June, we will visit my grandparents.

Sentence Patterns

A **phrase** is a group of related words that does not include its own subject and verb. A comma should follow an introductory phrase.

> <u>After dinner</u>, we will wash the dishes.
> <u>Laughing wildly</u>, the children tumbled down the hillside.
> <u>To prepare for the performance</u>, the class rehearsed every day.
> <u>A kind and funny boy</u>, Jason made friends easily.

A **clause** is a group of words that includes a subject and verb. There are two types of clauses: independent clauses and dependent clauses.

An **independent clause** can stand alone as a sentence. It tells a complete thought. In the following examples, each subject is underlined once, and each verb is underlined twice.

> The storm raged.
> We finished our homework early.
> The mother sang to the baby.

Although it includes both a subject and verb, a **dependent clause** cannot stand alone. It is not complete. Some dependent clauses begin with a relative pronoun, such as *who, whom, which,* or *that.* The relative pronoun may serve as the subject of the dependent clause. Other dependent clauses begin with a subordinating conjunction, such as *after, although, because, however, if, until,* and *when.* In the following examples, each subject is underlined once, and each verb is underlined twice.

> Until it was time for us to go.
> Because we started it sooner than usual.
> Who was crying.

On its own, none of these clauses (above) expresses a complete thought. It needs to be joined to an independent clause.

> The storm raged until it was time for us to go.
> Because we started it sooner than usual, we finished our homework early.
> The mother sang to the baby who was crying.

Different combinations of independent and dependent clauses form different types of sentences. There are four basic sentence patterns.

1. A **simple sentence** includes one independent clause and no dependent clauses.

   The ice cream melted.
   The girls sat together on the bus.
   Where are your keys?

2. A **compound sentence** includes two or more independent clauses combined using a coordinating conjunction. In the following examples, each independent clause is underlined.

   Andrew washed his jeans, but they were still stained with paint.
   Greg might go to Tim's house, or they will both go to the park.
   I brought the sandwiches, Fiona brought the salad, and Freddie brought the juice.

3. A **complex sentence** includes one independent clause and one or more dependent clauses combined using a subordinating conjunction. In the following examples, each independent clause is underlined once, and each dependent clause is underlined twice.

   I will wait for you if you want to come along.
   The baker who made these pies is famous for his lemon meringue.
   Because we have been working so hard, our teacher wants to know why we are not yet finished.

Notice that the dependent clause *who made these pies* appears between the subject and verb of the independent clause *The baker is famous for his lemon meringue.*

4. A **compound-complex sentence** includes two or more independent clauses and at least one dependent clause. In the following examples, each independent clause is underlined once, and each dependent clause is underlined twice.

   After they return home from school, Jumi walks the dog and Sung practices the piano.
   Please return the books that I left on the table to the library, and I will pay the fine when I go to the library next week.

Notice that the dependent clause *that I left on the table* appears before the prepositional phrase in the independent clause *Please return the books to the library.*

Notes

Notes

Notes

Notes

Notes